THE
HUNTER'S
HANDBOOK

THE HUNTER'S HANDBOOK

A guide to hunting in North America

By
Jerome J. Knap

Pagurian Press Limited
TORONTO

Printed and Bound in the United States
ISBN 0–88932–010–1

CONTENTS

Chapter

To my father —
still my favorite hunting partner

Introduction

Hunting is the bridge that spans the great expanse between the present and past when all men were hunters.

Fishing, whether most people realize it or not, is simply another form of hunting where the quarry is taken with a hook and line. At one time, spears, bows and arrows, and nets were used for taking all game, both fish and fowl alike.

Today, the physical need to hunt exists only among a few scattered bands of people in remote corners of the world. But the spiritual need to hunt, as well as the need to be out in the open spaces, exists in the souls of many men. A wildfowler hunting geese on the desolate coast of Hudson Bay is making a spiritual commitment to his origins; to his ancestors. He is re-creating the drama of life at its simplest.

Hunting involves the killing of game. There is no way the two can be separated. But the hunter's predatory skills depend on his skill in understanding his quarry and understanding the natural world around him. The hunter is a predator, interwoven into nature's web. A good hunter is also a good naturalist. These two are also inseparable.

This book is not intended to be a detailed treatise of hunting different species of game. This cannot be accomplished in one book. The book has been written as a handbook; a reference book on sporting firearms and North American game, with hints on where to find the game and how to hunt it.

Chapter I

Guns for the Game

The first firearms were developed in the 14th century as weapons of war. They were not particularly effective and historians have postulated that their military value came from the smoke and noise which at times terrified the enemy. The use of firearms for hunting began in Europe during the late 16th century with the invention of the wheel-lock. The evolution of firearms was spurred by hunters who generally accepted and used improvements in firearms long before the military.

RIFLES AND CARTRIDGES

The rifle gets its name from the fact that the bore of its barrel is rifled with grooves and lands. The purpose of the rifling is to control and direct the flight of the projectile — the bullet — during its flight by making the bullet spin. The rifling of a bore is not a new development. It was invented in Germany in the early 16th century. During the early years, the use of rifled firearms was confined almost exclusively to hunting.

The grooves and lands of the rifling vary in number, depth and width from one manufacturer to another. The pitch or twist of the rifling also varies from a rifle of one calibre to another. There is an optimum twist for every bullet weight and velocity at which it will be pushed up the barrel.

It is quite logical to consider the rifle barrel as a sort of internal combustion engine fueled by nitrocellulose gunpowder. The combustion or burning of this powder creates gases which exert pressure and push the bullet up the rifled bore from 0 to as much as 4140 feet per second. Simply speaking it is the amount and type of powder that determine how much pressure is built up in the bore. In turn, and again simply speaking, the amount of pressure created along with the weight of the bullet determine the speed at which the bullet will leave the muzzle of the barrel. Incidentally, modern smokeless gunpowder is a fuel or propellant, *not* an explosive as many people think.

TYPES OF RIFLES

There are basically two types of rifles — breech loading rifles in which the cartridge is inserted into the chamber of the rifle and fired, and muzzle loading rifles in which the powder is poured into the bore from the muzzle end and followed by a sealant or wadding and finally a bullet. Breech loading rifles are much newer in development and are universally used for both hunting and target shooting. Muzzle loading rifles, however, are enjoying a revival on the part of some hunters.

In breech loading rifles, there are six types of actions used — lever, bolt, slide, semi-automatic, single shot, and double barrelled. The lever, bolt, slide, and semi-automatic actions are the most popular.

Lever Action   The lever action is the oldest type of repeating rifle. It is one of the most popular types, particularly among deer hunters of the eastern forests. This is partially due to its reliability and because the lever action rifle is light, handy, allows fast successive shots, and can be used by both right- or left-handed shooters. The fact that it has been around for over a century has ingrained it in the minds of many hunters.

There are two essential types of lever actions. The older types such as the Winchester 94 and the Marlin 336 have exposed hammers, tubular magazines under the barrel, and are generally chambered for less intense cartridges such as the fine old .30-30 or the new .444 Marlin Magnum. The newer type of lever action such as the Savage 99 and the Winchester 88 have stronger actions and clip-type magazines. They shoot modern high intensity cartridges such as the .308 and .243 Winchester and the .300 Savage. The Browning lever action is a sort of hybrid between the other types of lever actions. It has an exposed hammer but has a clip-type box magazine. This very strong action is chambered for the modern higher powered cartridges. Lever action rifles are also made in the .22 rimfire cartridge for small game hunting.

Bolt Action   The bolt action rifles are generally considered to be more rugged, simpler, and more foolproof than the lever actions, and can take stronger pressures of high intensity cartridges. The bolt action rifle is the most accurate of all rifles, but successive shots cannot be fired as rapidly as with the other actions. The bolt action is made in a variety of styles, weights, and barrel lengths. Bolt actions are chambered for a greater variety of cartridges than any other rifle, from the .22 rimfire to the ponderous .460 Weatherby elephant rifle.

Winchester, Remington, Browning, Ruger, Savage, Weatherby, and a host of fine European firearms manufacturers make bolt action rifles. Most of these are modified Mauser types. Other types of bolt actions are the Manlicher, the Shultz and Larsen, and the new Colt Sauer.

Slide Action   The pump rifle is a fast, handy rifle especially useful where

10

fast successive shots are frequently needed. The slide action rifles have their following, but they are not as popular as the bolt action or the lever. They are probably not even as popular as the semi-automatic. Slide action rifles have never achieved the popularity of the pump shotgun. Slide action big game rifles are made by Remington and Savage. Slide action rifles are chambered for cartridges from the .22 rimfire to the .30,06.

Semi-Automatic Action   The semi-automatic rifles are at least as popular as the pump in the case of centerfire cartridges. However, in the .22 rimfire, the automatic may very well be the most popular of the actions. The modern semi-automatic rifles are light and reliable. They are preferred by hunters who want a second or third shot quickly. Semi-automatic rifles have slightly softer recoil than the other action types with rifles of the same weight and chambered for the same cartridge. This is due to some of the gas from the powder being used to "power" the action. In big game cartridges, semi-automatics are made by Remington, Winchester, and Browning.

Other Actions   Single shot rifles were very popular before the turn of the century. Today, aside from inexpensive single shots in .22 rimfire, two very fine single shot big game rifles are available on the market — the Ruger and the Hyper. Both are very expensive and generally of interest only to the nuttier of gun nuts. Harrington and Richards also makes an inexpensive single shot in the popular .30-30 as well as a number of military replicas of the 1871 Springfield in .45-70. Single shot rifles have the advantage of overall shortness because there is no action as such. Thus the single shot rifle can have a very long barrel for maximum velocity and still be a short, handy rifle.

Double barrelled rifles, both side-by-side and over-and-under, are also available. The side-by-side doubles are generally English and usually chambered for big cartridges for the dangerous game of Africa. They are considered to be the finest examples of the gun making art. The over-and-unders are usually German or Austrian and are chambered for lighter cartridges. All double rifles, particularly the side-by-side, are expensive and are rarely encountered. Some double barrelled rifles are still made today.

CARTRIDGES

Cartridges are divided into two basic groups — rimfire and centerfire. Rimfire cartridges were invented first. They are not very powerful and are used for small game or for plinking and target shooting. Today, only rifles for the .22 rimfire, the .22 Winchester rimfire magnum, and the 5 mm Remington are being made. However, .25 and .32 rimfire cartridges are still loaded for older rifles. The centerfire cartridges are made in numerous calibres from .22 for varmint hunting through the .460 Weatherby for elephants and other African big game.

The difference between these two types of cartridges, aside from size, is the method by which the powder is ignited. In the rimfire, the priming compound lies around the entire rim. When the firing pin strikes the rim, the powder ignites and the bullet is pushed out the barrel. In the centerfire, the priming compound is in a primer or cap in the center of the cartridge base. The brass case of the centerfire cartridge is a great deal stronger than the case of the rimfire and hence can be loaded with more intense powder charges. Rimfire cartridges are much less expensive. However, centerfire cartridge cases can be reloaded with a new primer, powder, and a new bullet. Hand loading ammunition has become a popular hobby with many shooters. Hand loading can save money, but it also allows the hand loader to custom craft a load that is more accurate for his rifle than factory loaded ammunition.

Choosing the best cartridge for the game is not difficult. The following tables will be of help in selecting the best cartridge and bullet weight for the various species of big game.

Cartridges for Medium-Sized Game
(deer, sheep, pronghorn, goat, black bear)

Cartridge	Bullet Wgt. (grs.)	Velocity (f.p.s.) Muzzle	Velocity (f.p.s.) 100 yds.	Energy (ft.-lbs.) Muzzle	Energy (ft.-lbs.) 100 yds.
.243 Winchester............	100	3070	2790	2090	1730
.244 Remington............	90	3200	2850	2050	1630
6 mm Remington	100	3190	2920	2260	1890
.240 Weatherby...........	100	3395	3115	2554	2150
.257 Weatherby...........	117	3300	2900	2824	2184
.264 Winchester...........	140	3200	2940	3180	2690
6.5 mm Remington Mag. ...	120	3030	2750	2450	2010
.270 Winchester...........	130	3140	2850	2840	2340
.270 Winchester...........	150	2800	2400	2610	1920
.280 Remington...........	150	2810	2580	2630	2220
*.280 Remington...........	165	2770	2460	2810	2220
.284 Winchester...........	150	2900	2630	2800	2300
*7 mm Mauser	175	2490	2170	2410	1830
7 mm Remington Mag.	150	3260	2950	3540	2900
*30-30	150	2410	2020	1930	1360
*.30-30	170	2220	1890	1860	1350
.30-'06....................	180	2700	2470	2910	2440
.300 Win. Magnum	150	3400	3050	3850	3100
.300 Win. Magnum	180	3070	2850	3770	3250
.300 Weatherby...........	150	3545	3195	4179	3393
.300 Weatherby...........	180	3245	2960	4201	3501
*.300 Savage	150	2670	2390	2370	1900
*.300 Savage	180	2370	2160	2240	1860
*.308 Winchester...........	150	2860	2570	2730	2200
*.308 Winchester...........	180	2610	2390	2720	2280
.303 British	150	2720	2420	2460	1950
.303 British	180	2540	2180	2580	1900
*.32 Win. Special	170	2280	1870	1960	1320
*.35 Remington...........	150	2400	1960	1920	1280
*.35 Remington...........	200	2210	1830	2170	1490
*.358 Winchester...........	200	2530	2210	2840	2160
*.350 Rem. Magnum	200	2710	2410	3260	2570
*.444 Marlin	240	2400	1845	3070	1815
*.44 Magnum	240	1850	1450	1820	1120

best for short range hunting in woods

12

Cartridge	Bullet Wgt. (grs.)	Velocity (f.p.s.) Muzzle	Velocity (f.p.s.) 100 yds.	Energy (ft.-lbs.) Muzzle	Energy (ft.-lbs.) 100 yds.
.270 Winchester............	150	2800	2400	2610	1920
.280 Remington............	165	2770	2460	2810	2220
7 mm Remington Mag......	175	3020	2670	3540	2770
.30-'06...................	180	2700	2470	2910	2440
.30-'06...................	220	2410	2180	2830	2320
.280 Remington...........	165	2770	2460	2810	2220
.308 Winchester...........	200	2450	2210	2670	2170
.303 British	180	2540	2180	2580	1900
.303 British	215	2180	1900	2270	1720
.300 Winchester Mag.	180	3070	2850	3770	3250
.300 Winchester Mag.	220	2720	2490	3620	3030
.300 H&H Magnum........	180	2920	2670	3400	2850
.300 H&H Magnum........	220	2620	2370	3350	2740
.300 Weatherby...........	180	3245	2960	4201	3501
.300 Weatherby...........	220	2905	2610	4123	3329
.338 Winchester Mag.	200	3000	2690	4000	3210
.338 Winchester Mag.	250	2700	2430	4050	3280
.338 Winchester Mag.	300	2450	2160	4000	3110
.340 Weatherby...........	200	3210	2905	4566	3748
.340 Weatherby...........	250	2850	2580	4510	3695
.350 Remington Mag.	250	2410	2190	3220	2660
.375 H&H Magnum........	270	2740	2460	4500	3620
.375 H&H Magnum........	300	2550	2280	4330	3460

HUNTING SIGHTS

Three types of rifle sights are available — open, aperture or peep, and telescopic. The standard sights on hunting rifles shipped straight from the factory are open sights. The front sight is usually a bead — red, white, or gold — and the rear sight is a metal element set into a slot in the barrel with a "U" or "V" notch cut into it for the actual aiming. Open sights are suitable for short ranges. They are fine for young shooters whose nimble eyes can focus on three separate objects — the rear sight, the bead, and the target — very quickly. Open sights are not good for older hunters whose eyes are less keen.

Aperture sights consist of a hole in the center of a disc attached to an adjustable base. The aperture sight is mounted back on the receiver of the rifle, close to the eye. The shooter looks through the sight, *not* at it. The eye then focuses only on two objects, the bead of the front sight and the target. The elevation and windage are adjusted by micro-meter knobs on the sight.

Aperture sights are much more accurate than open sights. This is why they are used on all target rifles. However, what most hunters don't realize is that aperture sights are also very fast. The secret lies in the big aperture (¼ of an inch or thereabouts) so that the eye finds the aperture immediately upon shouldering the rifle. Both open and aperture sights are sometimes collectively called iron sights.

The telescopic sight is the finest of all rifle sights. It has several virtues. The magnification of the 'scope helps the shooter to see better, a distinct advantage in more accurate shooting. The 'scope's light gathering qualities allow the hunter to shoot earlier at dawn and later at dusk by a good half hour. This is extremely important because big game move about mostly at twilight. Also, when using a 'scope, the shooter focuses only on the target. The 'scope's reticle, which can be a crosshair, a post, or a dot, is super-imposed over or on the target.

Today, the modern rifle 'scope is a tough instrument, almost as rugged as any other sight. The secret of using a 'scope lies in the selection and mounting. Too many hunters equate the magnifying power with always being a good thing, when at times too much power is a handicap. For woods shooting, low-powered 'scopes — 1½ to 2½ power — are best. Lower pow-ered 'scopes have wide fields of view. This simply means that they take in more area. These are the 'scopes to use for fast moving targets at close range — deer, moose, and elk in the woods. For big game in more open country and mountains, a moderately powered 'scope such as 4 power is best. For long range plains shooting, a 6 power is preferred by some hunters. The very high-powered 'scopes — 8 power to 12 power — are only for 'chucks and other stationary varmints and target shooting.

'Scopes are attached to rifles by mounts. Some mounts are detachable or hinged for easy removal of the 'scope. These are the best choice for big game rifles in case the 'scope gets damaged or is put out of commission because of fog. In such situations the hunter can use his iron sights. There are two types of mounts — top and side. The top mount fits onto bases that are attached to the rifle. Most rifles are tapped and drilled for easy attachment of 'scope mount bases. A few rifles now have built-in bases. The rings or the bridge that hold the 'scope are mounted onto the bases. The bridge-type of mount is one of the strongest, the most rigid. The side mount fits onto the side of the rifle's receiver. The side mount is very re-liable and is preferred by some hunters because of this. But since it requires mounting by a gunsmith, it is not as popular as the top mount. All 'scopes should be mounted low so that when the rifle is at the shoulder, the shooter's eye is level with the 'scope.

THE SLING

A good sling is an invaluable accessory for any rifle. A sling is a must when dragging a deer out of the bush. It takes the drudgery out of carrying the rifle over long distances. The sling is worth its weight in gold when climbing mountains after sheep or goats. It is a big help in keeping the rifle steady when shooting prone or sitting. Slings should be attached to rifles by means of detachable swivels so that they can be removed when the rifle is used in brush. I wouldn't be without a good sling on any of my rifles.

14

RIFLES FOR MOUNTAINS, FORESTS, PLAINS, and VARMINTS

Rifles are classified by the type of hunting for which they will be used. A compromise, an "all around" rifle, also exists.

The mountain rifle must be very accurate and chambered for flat-shooting cartridges because the ranges can be long. The cartridge depends on the game. For sheep, a .25,06 is fine, but if grizzly will also be hunted, the cartridge should be at least a .270. The rifle must be light because it will be carried a great deal while climbing. Its ideal barrel length is about 22 inches and it should not exceed 24 inches because the rifle then becomes too unwieldy. It should have a 'scope sight of moderate power, 4 power perhaps being the best. The bolt action is generally the preferred rifle type for the mountains.

The plains rifle must have some of the same attributes as the mountain rifle. The ranges for plains game such as pronghorns tend to be very long, so the rifle must be very accurate and flat-shooting. Because plains game are not very big and tough, the cartridges need not be too powerful. Anything from the .243 or 6 mm range to the .30 calibres with 150 grain bullets would be a good choice. The rifle does not have to be as light as the mountain rifle because the hunter does not climb. The barrel can even be 26 inches, but 24 inches is better. The plains rifle should have a 'scope sight of 4 power, with 6 power at times being very useful.

The woods rifle should be fairly light, well balanced, and easy to handle for fast shooting at close range. Exceptionally fine-edged accuracy is not needed. For forest game such as white-tailed or black-tailed deer, the rifle can be chambered for a much lighter calibre. The old .30-30 is fine. If moose and elk are also hunted, then the rifle must be chambered for a more powerful cartridge — the .308 or .30,06. The sights can be anything the hunter prefers or is used to, but there is no doubt that a 'scope of 1½ or 2½ power is the best. The critical thing is that the stock fit the shooter perfectly so that when the rifle is shouldered, the eye is level with the scope.

The all around rifle for big game is not difficult to choose. The action is irrelevant. If the preference lies with the bolt action, pump, or semi-automatic, the best calibre is still the .30,06. If you prefer a lever action, then the calibre must be .308. The .270 Winchester, .280 Remington, and the 7 mm Remington magnum are also very good. The rifle should be scope sighted with a 3-power or a variable power 'scope such as a 1½-4½ or a 2-7. The rifle should not be too heavy, a maximum of 8 pounds. If varmints will also be hunted with this all around rifle, then the best choice would be a bolt action in .270 Winchester or .280 Remington with a variable 'scope of 3 to 9 power.

The varmint rifle is a specialized rifle. For long range shooting on stationary targets such as woodchucks and rockchucks, the rifle should have a long heavy barrel for maximum velocity and peak accuracy. The best calibres are .222, .22-250, .243 Winchester, 6 mm Remington, and .25-06. The rifle should have an 8 to 12 power scope. In farm country where noise is a problem and ranges are shorter, a .222 Remington is the best. The varmint rifle must be very accurate, because a 'chuck at 200 yards is not a large target. An 8 power 'scope is the best sight. For other varmints such as running jackrabbits or coyotes, any flat-shooting big game rifle with a 4 power 'scope is a good bet. The ideal cartridges for coyotes are .243 Winchester, 6 mm Remington, and the .25,06.

The small game rifle will be used largely on gray squirrels, but also possibly on cottontails and snowshoe hares. Tack driving accuracy is not needed for bunnies bouncing through thick cover. However, a fast second or third shot is needed. The semi-automatics, pumps, and lever actions are the best bet for rabbits. For gray squirrels, fine accuracy is needed. A squirrel pressed against a tree trunk 50 yards away is not an easy target. The best squirrel rifle is a good quality bolt action with a 4 power scope.

SHOOTING THE RIFLE

The key to success with rifles lies in shooting skill. No one can be an accurate shot without practice. This is one of the reasons why the average deer hunter is a bum shot. He doesn't practice enough.

A myth persists among some hunters that certain people have instinctive shooting abilities. Target shooters know better. They know very well that good shots are made and not born. It is true that some people have better eyesight and better muscular coordination. Such people become good shots quickly, but they still need to be made — trained.

A hunter who gets his buck each season may fancy himself a good shot, but that may not be the case. The fact may be that a freckle-faced, 14-year-old on a high school rifle team can shoot rings around him. A deer is a pretty big target.

The key factors in shooting a rifle well are mundane and simple. The rifle must be held as steady as possible. Even on a moving target, the rifle must be swung smoothly without wobbles or jerks, and the shot must be let off without disturbing the aim. This means squeezing the trigger — gently but firmly. An experienced rifleman knows where his sights were resting the instant the shot went off. This is called "calling the shot". It is indispensable in becoming a good shot.

There are four orthodox shooting positions which have been developed over many generations by skilled riflemen. These form the basis of fine rifle shooting. They are not equally useful in the field, but once mastered, they make a good rifle shot.

The four positions are as follows:

Prone In this position the body should be at about 45 degrees with a line of aim. The legs should be well spread with the insides of both feet flat on the ground. The spine should be straight and the upper part of the body supported by the triangle formed by the trunk and the upper arms. The heel of the left hand should be well under the forearm of the rifle and neither hand should grip too tightly. If properly positioned, the bones rather than the muscles should be doing most of the work of holding the gun in position.

Sitting In the sitting position, the face should be almost half right again, but the body should lean forward until the elbows are braced over the knees. Again, the left elbow should be well under the rifle. As in the prone position, the body forms a good tripod base. Feet and legs can be spread or together or the ankles may be crossed according to preference. Remember that neither the knees nor thighs must touch the ground. The eye, as in all shooting positions, should be kept as close to the rear sight as possible.

Kneeling Kneeling is more difficult than either the prone or sitting positions, and you should have a fair amount of practice with it before attempting it in the field.

Again, face half right and get down on the right knee, sitting on either the heel or the inside of the right foot. The left elbow should rest on the left knee well under the barrel. The right elbow should be held as high as possible with comfort. This position is difficult to hold for any length of time, and there is a tendency to sway. The more comfortable you can make yourself, the longer you will be able to maintain this position.

Standing Body support in the standing position is at a minimum. It is therefore almost impossible to hold the rifle absolutely steady. The important object is to keep the movement of the barrel to a minimum. The shooter stands with feet spread, the right elbow about shoulder high or above, and the left arm well under the forearm. The butt of the stock is higher on the shoulder than in any of the other positions. There are slight variations of this position.

SHOOTING IN THE FIELD

Experienced big game hunters always use the steadiest position possible. They lean into a handy tree trunk or cushion a rock with a hat or jacket to use as a rest. They prefer the prone, sitting, and kneeling positions in that order over the standing position. They use the rifle sling for shooting support whenever possible.

Shooting skill is an important part of hunting skill. Repeated tests by armed forces have demonstrated that the majority of men cannot tolerate more than 18 pounds of recoil from their rifles and still shoot well. What is the piece of wisdom behind this knowledge? Stay away from light rifles in big magnum calibres. If you feel you need a magnum, get a heavier rifle.

SHOTGUNS AND LOADS

The shotgun is a smooth-bored weapon. It is primarily used for hunting game birds and small game mammals. With buckshot or slugs, it can be used for big game. The shotgun barrel, like the rifle barrel, is also an internal combustion engine fueled by nitrocellulose powder. Its basic function is to accelerate a mass of tiny spherical pellets — shot — from 0 up to, in some case, 1330 feet per second, and to direct the mass of shot towards a clay target or game bird. The flight of the shot is controlled with a constriction at the muzzle known as the "choke".

TYPES OF SHOTGUNS

As in the case of rifles, there are basic types of shotguns — breech loaders and muzzle loaders. Again, breech loading shotguns are much newer. The first practical breech loading shotgun was developed in France during the middle of the last century. Breech loading shotguns are universally used for both hunting and target shooting; that is, skeet or trap. Hunting with muzzle loading guns is also enjoying a bit of a revival by some black powder shooters.

There are six shotgun types — the double barrel, the slide action or pump, the semi-automatic, the bolt action, the single barrel or single shot, and the lever action.

Double-Barrelled Shotguns There are two types of double-barrelled shotguns — the "over-and-under" and the "side-by-side". In over-and-under shotguns, the two barrels are joined so that one is on top of the other. In the classic side-by-side double, the barrels are joined together horizontally. At the turn of the century, side-by-side doubles dominated the shotgun market. Their popularity fell with the introduction of the repeating shotguns. However, today the side-by-side is making a strong comeback as a prestige gun. Some of the side-by-side doubles certainly represent the best of the gun making art.

The over-and-under has risen in popularity since the 1920's, and today is one of the most popular of the higher priced shotguns. The single sighting plane gives it an advantage in clay pigeon shooting over the side-by-side.

Double barrelled guns have some advantages over other types of shotguns. The two barrels give an instant selection of two different chokes, either for short or longer ranges. Since there is no action, double barrelled shotguns are several inches shorter than the pumps or semi-automatics with the same barrel length. To many shooters, this makes doubles somewhat handier, faster swinging, and better balanced. Most doubles have their safety catch on the tang — the handiest place for a safety.

Good quality side-by-side doubles are made in Italy and Spain, but the best are made in Britain by Holland and Holland, Purdey, Churchill, and others. Fine doubles were at one time made in the United States by such firms as Parker, L. C. Smith, and Fox. The model 21 Winchester is the last of these top quality doubles made in the United States. Good over-and-unders are made in several countries — in Germany, Italy, and Japan by Winchester and Ithaca, and one of the best is the Browning made in Belgium.

The Slide Action The slide action or pump shotgun is a rugged, relatively inexpensive, and easy to repair gun. It is strictly an American invention. It is rarely encountered anywhere else in the world. Most pumps hold five shells, one in the chamber and four in the magazine, but for waterfowl shooting they must be plugged to three shells in total, by law.

Pump shotguns are made by nearly all the leading manufacturers of sporting arms. They are made in various styles and in all gauges. For a man who wants a more versatile gun, spare barrels are relatively inexpensive for pump guns or a choke device can be installed on the barrel of the pump.

Slide action shotguns are longer than doubles with the same barrel length because of the action. This, to some gunners, makes them somewhat more poorly balanced and less handy. They are a little more rattly. The critics of pump guns say that they are mere machines, not works of the gun making art as are doubles. That may well be, but pumps sure have bagged a lot of game.

The Autoloader The semi-automatic or autoloading shotgun, is not really new. It has been around for almost as long as the pump; however, the early models were heavy, clumsy affairs and not very popular. This has changed. The autoloaders now have become light, sleek, and attractive. Their design and engineering have vastly improved, and today they are rapidly gaining in popularity. In fact, in some fields they have overtaken the pump.

The semi-automatic is one of the most foolproof of shotguns. An excited shooter may jam a pump gun by not pumping back far enough. However, with an automatic this cannot happen. All the gunner has to do is pull the trigger. It is the recoil in the older types of automatics and the gas generated from the combustion of the gunpowder in the modern automatics that works the action and ejects the fired shell, bringing a fresh shell into the firing chamber.

In the gas-operated autoloaders such as the Remington 1100 and the Winchester 1400, the operation of the action absorbs about 30 percent of the recoil. This has endeared the automatic to all who are bothered by the "kick" of guns and to trap and skeet shooters who do a lot of shooting in the course of a day. As the years go by, the semi-automatic will take over more and more of the market that was once dominated by the pump.

The Bolt Action The bolt action shotgun is a cheap and rugged gun. It is generally looked upon as a boy's gun or a utility gun for the farm. Although bolt action shotguns are repeaters, getting off a second shot at a duck or pheasant is all but impossible. This type of action is just too slow for birds on the wing. Consequently, the bolt action is generally not used by serious bird hunters. What keeps them on the market is their low price. In areas where shotguns must be used on deer, bolt action shotguns with cut down barrels and good sights or even 'scopes are used by many hunters. Some manufacturers have special slug models.

The Single Shot The single barrelled gun is the most inexpensive of all shotguns. It is the best bet for a youngster learning to shoot. It is safe, and because it has only one shot, the shooter tries to make that one shot count. This can help to make him a better hunter. The single barrelled shotgun can be had with or without a hammer. I would always recommend the hammerless type because a hammer can be very difficult for a young boy to pull back. Many single shot shotguns are light and very well balanced. They are made in a variety of gauges.

The Lever Action No lever action shotguns are made today, but Winchester has made two different models in 12 and 10 gauges. Both are interesting as collector's items. The lever action can shoot faster than the bolt action, but not as fast as the pump or the others.

UNDERSTANDING THE CHOKE

The shotgun choke is the source of much misunderstanding among shooters. It is a constriction at the muzzle that controls the mass of shot being fired. The choke actually works something like an adjustable nozzle on a garden hose. The mass of pellets being pushed forward up the barrel by the wads ahead of the expanding powder gases is similar to water being pushed up the hose. When the shot charge is pushed through the choke or constriction, the pellets are jammed together into a mass. They squirt from the muzzle in a brief stream. Basically, the tighter the constriction, the more massed the pellets become and the further the gun will shoot. But in practice, there is such a thing as overconstriction or overchoking in the garden hose, as well as in the shotgun barrel. When the nozzle on the hose is overconstricted, the water will spray out. The same thing can happen in an overchoked shotgun.

Chokes are named and categorized on the basis of the pattern they shoot into a 30-inch circle at 40 yards. The pattern is calculated by the number of shot holes in this 30-inch circle and worked out as a percentage of the charge, that is, the total number of shot pieces in the type of shotgun shell being used. The chapter on patterning a shotgun covers this in more detail.

A full choke shoots the tightest pattern and therefore is used for long range shotgunning. Waterfowl guns are generally full-choked. Improved cylinder guns shoot broader patterns. They are therefore used on upland game birds in woods where the ranges will be short. Because the pattern is broader, it makes hitting at close ranges easier.

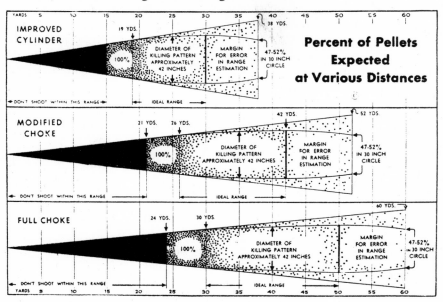

GAUGES AND LOADS

The system of referring to shotguns by gauges started many years ago. The gun's bore was designated by the number of specific round balls of pure lead (to the pound) that fit into the bore. For example, the bore of a 12 gauge gun is .730 inches, with 12 identical round lead balls weighing one pound. The bore diameter of a 10 gauge barrel is .775 inches, a 16 gauge

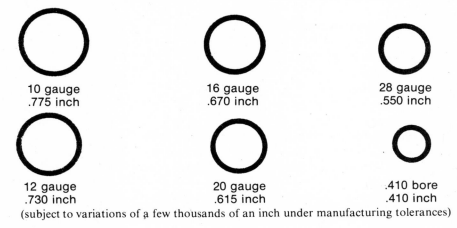

10 gauge
.775 inch

16 gauge
.670 inch

28 gauge
.550 inch

12 gauge
.730 inch

20 gauge
.615 inch

.410 bore
.410 inch

(subject to variations of a few thousands of an inch under manufacturing tolerances) barrel is .670 inches, a 20 gauge barrel is .615 inches, a 28 gauge barrel is .550 inches. The .410 gauge is the only departure from the system. It would more properly be called the .410 bore.

Shotguns were designed to fire a mass of pellets. These can number from several hundred to an ounce in the case of No. 9 shot to eight pellets per ounce in the case of No. 00 buckshot sizes. There are now some new shotgun barrels on the market specially designed for shooting a single rifled slug for deer.

The following is a table of the various shot sizes:

Size of Shot	Diameter in Inches	Pellets per Ounce
9	.08	585
8	.09	410
7½	.09½	350
6	.11	225
5	.12	170
4	.13	135
2	.15	90
BB	.18	50

Shotgun shells are loaded with a variety of loads. The powder is always expressed in "drams equivalent". In the early days of black powder, the powder charge was measured in drams. There are 16 drams to an ounce. Today's smokeless powder is more "powerful", thus a smaller amount of it achieves the same muzzle velocity and pressure as a greater amount of black powder. The term 3 drams equivalent simply means that the smokeless powder in a shell is equivalent to 3 drams of black powder.

Shotgun shells are loaded with various dram equivalents and various weights of shot charges. For example, the 2¾ inch 12 gauge shotgun shell can be obtained with 1⅛ ounces of shot and 2¾ drams equivalent, or 1¼ ounces of shot and 3¾ drams equivalent of powder. These loads are respectively called light loads and heavy loads. The extra heavy loads are called magnums. The designations describing the amount of shot, drams equivalent, and the shot size are written: 1⅛ — 3 — 7½.

Shotgun shells are made in various lengths with 2¾ inches being the standard in North America. However, the 12, 20, and the .410 bore are also made in a 3-inch length. The standard .410 is 2½ inches long, while the 10 gauge is also made in 3½ inches. The length is always measured with the crimp open after firing.

The following table gives the loads and velocities of various shotgun shells:

Gauge	Length	Powder Chg. Drs. Equiv.	Oz. Shot	Muzzle Velocity
12	2¾"	2¾	1⅛	1145
12	2¾"	3	1	1235
12	2¾"	3	1⅛	1200

12	2¾″	3¼	1⅛	1255
12	2¾″	3¼	1¼	1220
12	2¾″	3¾	1¼	1330
12	2¾″ Mag.	4	1½	1315
12	3″ Mag.	4¼	1⅝	1315
12	3″ Mag.	4½	1⅞	1255
16	2¾″	2½	1	1165
16	2¾″	2¾	1⅛	1185
16	2¾″	3	1⅛	1240
16	2¾″	3¼	1⅛	1295
16	2¾″ Mag.	3½	1¼	1295
20	2¾″	2½	⅞	1155
20	2¾″	2½	1	1165
20	2¾″	2¾	1	1220
20	2¾″ Mag.	3	1⅛	1220
20	3″ Mag.	3¼	1¼	1220
28	2¾″	2¼	¾	1295
28	2¾″ Mag.	2¾	1	1220
.410	3″	Max.	¾	1135
.410	2½″	Max.	½	1135

CHOOSING A SHOTGUN

Shotguns are generally selected on the basis of what game they will be used on and are categorized as upland game guns and wildfowl or duck guns. This division is largely because the requirements of a gun for these two types of game are different. There is also a compromise situation where one shotgun can be used on all game. The action type — pump, autoloader, side-by-side, or over-and-under — is solely dictated by personal preference and price.

UPLAND GAME GUNS

A gun for upland game hunting should be light to carry. The hunter walks a great deal, frequently the entire day. Many species of upland game live in woodlots and thick cover where the ranges, by necessity, are always short. Even the upland game which live in open fields are generally shot at short ranges, certainly shorter than waterfowl ranges. So the upland game gun should be choked for good pattern spread and should be short-barrelled for fast swinging. Light guns also tend to be fast swinging.

Shotgun shells with light loads are usually adequate. The only exceptions may be pheasants or sharp-tailed grouse when the birds are flushing wild in the late season. For such gunning a tighter choke and long range loads are preferable.

For more specialized upland game gunning, such as band-tailed pigeons as they swoop down through mountain passes or wild turkeys, both of which are generally shot at longer ranges, the gun should shoot tight patterns.

The preferred gauges are 12, 16, and 20. Many upland game hunters prefer the 20 gauge for the uplands, particularly in thick cover, because the guns are lighter and trimmer. Smaller gauges — 28 and .410 — are guns for the expert wing shot. Hunting with them is much more difficult. They are frequently given to a beginner, a boy, or a woman, because they are light and have light recoil, but this is wrong. They make hitting difficult, which discourages the beginner.

DUCK GUNS

The ranges at which waterfowl tend to be killed are generally considerably longer than those in the uplands. This requires guns with tight chokes and shells with heavier or even magnum loads. Because heavier loads are used, waterfowl guns should be heavier than upland bird guns or the recoil after much shooting will be unpleasant. Since waterfowl hunting seldom involves much walking, the weight of the gun is not an important factor.

A compromise between a light upland game gun and a heavy waterfowl gun is a medium weight shotgun with a moderate barrel length. It should have a variable choke device or a spare barrel, one full-choked and the other improved cylinder.

Here are some choke recommendations for different types of game:

— Improved cylinder: ruffed and blue grouse, quail, woodcock, cottontails, pheasants and huns in the early season when they are still holding well, snipe when they are holding well, ptarmigan.

— Modified choke: ducks over decoys, doves, sage grouse, sharptails in the early season when they are still holding well, pheasants and huns in the late season when they are flushing further.

— Full choke: ducks, geese, turkeys, band-tailed pigeons, sharptails and snipe in the late season when they are flushing further.

The following table gives recommendations on the best shot size and type of load for various species of game:

	Shot Size
Waterfowl Shooting:	
duck shooting over decoys (heavy loads)	5 or 6
all other duck shooting (magnum loads)	4
goose shooting (magnum loads)	BB, 2, or 4
Upland Game Shooting:	
snipe, woodcock, and rails (light loads)	7½, 8, or 9
doves, pigeons, quail, crows (light loads)	7½ or 8
ruffed grouse, cottontails, huns, squirrels (light loads)	6 or 7½
pheasants, sharptails, prairie chickens, blue grouse, snowshoe hare (heavy loads)	5 or 6
turkeys, foxes, jackrabbits (heavy or magnum loads)	2 or 4
skeet shooting (skeet loads)	8 or 9
trap shooting (trap loads)	7½ or 8

SHOOTING A SHOTGUN

There are three basic techniques for shooting a shotgun. Each technique has an advantage for a particular set of circumstances. An experienced shotgunner instinctively uses the best technique for that particular shot. This instinctive selection of shooting technique comes only with a great deal of shooting experience. Every shotgunner knows that you must lead a moving target, shoot ahead of it, so that the mass of shot and the target meet. However, all shotgunners do not consciously lead their targets.

The "swing through" system is the most commonly used for upland game shooting. In this technique, the barrel is tracked along the flight path of the bird. As the barrel overtakes and passes the bird, the gunner shoots, but continues to swing with the bird. Continuing the swing is important. It helps to produce the correct lead without the gunner's having to calculate it. If the swing is stopped immediately upon shooting, a miss will occur as the result of underleading.

"Snap" or "spot" shooting is another system used by hunters. In this technique, the gun is quickly pointed and fired at a spot ahead of the bird so that the shot and the bird meet. This technique is used for very close range shooting in thick cover where there is not much time because the target will soon be gone. Grouse and woodcock hunters use it. It requires accurate timing and lightning fast reflexes for good results.

The "sustained lead" is the third method of shooting a shotgun. With this technique the gunner picks a spot ahead of the bird, tracks the barrel ahead of the bird, and sustains a certain amount of lead at all times, so that when he shoots the bird and shot will meet. This shooting technique requires more time to implement. The bird has to be in the open. It is the best technique for pass shooting waterfowl.

To shoot a shotgun well, the gun must fit the gunner and not vice versa. Generally speaking, the beginning gunner of average height and build can be certain that any currently made factory shotgun will fit him reasonably well. It was designed that way. However, if you are a big chap, you will need a longer stock; one with longer pull. And vice versa if you are a gunner of smaller stature as many men and most women are. If the butt of the stock catches on your clothes as you shoulder the gun or if you have to stretch, the stock is too long. However, a lot of other things enter into a good gun fit.

The problems of shotgun fit can be remedied by a good gunsmith. The problem is to learn what is wrong. A good gunsmith or stock maker again may be of help. He can tell a great deal by watching you shoulder your gun. Similarly, a shooting coach or a very experienced shotgunner at a skeet or trap club can also be helpful.

All hunters should practice on clay birds regularly. Skeet is generally best for upland game practice and trap for waterfowl. If you have shooting bugs due to bad gunning habits or poor stock fit, the skeet and trap range with an experienced shot watching is a good place to learn what the problems are. Don't be shy. Just go ahead and ask for help. You will never be turned down.

SHOOTING BUGS

Flinching is a problem that frequently crops up to put a bug into shooting. Flinching is a nervous reaction triggered by the shot. It is caused by the recoil and/or the muzzle blast. Many shooters don't even know when they are flinching. The recoil of the gun hides it. But if you squeeze the trigger on a gun with an empty chamber when you thought it was loaded, you'll feel yourself jerk or shudder. Usually someone watching you shoot can also determine if you are flinching.

Only when you know you are flinching can you start doing something about it. First, switch to a smaller calibre. Use a .270 instead of a .300 magnum or a 20 gauge instead of a 12. This decreases the recoil. Switch from a 7½ pound featherweight to a 9 pounder. This also decreases recoil. Switch to softer loads in shotguns — field loads instead of long range loads — and to a gas-operated semi-automatic. This will also lessen the recoil.

Use earplugs of some sort, the muff type being the best. Earplugs lessen the muzzle blast and thus help to lessen the flinch.

My last advice is to try coping with flinching on the psychological level. Try to "will yourself" not to flinch. This is difficult, but some shooters can do it, at least sometimes.

Console yourself that most shooters are afflicted with it at one point or another. It is almost like death and taxes. Flinching is very common in the overgunned hunter.

Hearing protection is another aspect of shooting that deserves consideration. Heavily repeated exposure to the sound of shotguns, high power rifles and handguns causes permanent hearing damage. Usually this hearing loss is not discovered until it's too late.

Hearing guards are one piece of equipment that every shooter should have. They are not practical for hunting, but for sharpening shooting skills on the range, they are a must. There are a number of different types of hearing guards on the market. The inexpensive plug or insert type are the least efficient. The muff type are the best, but some shotgunners have difficulty shooting with them because they interfere with the mounting of the gun. For these shooters, custom molded, insert-type hearing guards are the best bet.

Aside from protecting your hearing against damage, hearing guards also contribute to shooting accuracy. Repeated tests have proven that shooters shoot better with hearing guards than without.

Chapter II

Dogs for the Game

A good hunting dog is easily the most valuable hunting companion a man can have. Watching a dog plunge into icy water to retrieve a duck, come to a snappy point on a big cock pheasant, or course through a "birdy" cover is an important part of hunting. Many of us get almost as much pleasure out of our dogs as we do out of shooting. And aside from the joys and aesthetics that a dog contributes to a day in the marsh or the uplands, the dog also ensures a heavier game bag and promotes wise use of our wildlife resources by retrieving all downed game.

Choosing a hunting dog can be difficult, particularly for the tyro hunter. Choosing a dog is a double-barrelled problem. The first choice to be made is the type and breed of dog. The second is the actual choice of a puppy from a litter or the choice between a puppy and a trained dog. The type of game hunted, the space available for the dog at home, and even family preferences are important in making the first choice. Time, dog training experience and even temperament are important in making the second.

POINTING DOGS

The task of a pointing or "bird" dog is to search out birds, point them staunchly, remain on point until the hunter flushes, shoots the birds and reloads, and ideally to retrieve on command. For these purposes, the English setter and the pointer are hard to beat, They are upland bird specialists. The term "bird dogs" describes them well.

The pointing dog who does not carry out the complete task described above is not fully trained. It's most desirable to have a dog fully trained, because the dog who breaks to shot may begin breaking to wing, even if it's only because he wants to be the first to retrieve. From there it's a down-hill slide until the dog begins flushing birds before the hunter has a chance to approach for a shot. The dog is then next to useless.

During the early season, pheasants, grouse, and quail are still in family coveys. Since not all the birds flush together, the dog who breaks to shot in order to retrieve or to chase the birds will flush the remaining birds before the hunter is able to reload. There is always the added bonus that if your dog is fully trained, he can compete in any field trial and have a chance to win.

RETRIEVERS

A retriever sits to shot, marks a fallen bird, and then retrieves from land or water. The fully trained dog must also be able to follow a "line" or hand signals to locate a bird he has not marked. These are the basic requirements for a retriever competing in a field trial, but a blind retrieve is also valuable in the duck marsh because the dog is rarely capable of simultaneously marking three or four downed birds. Wing-tipped birds may also land far out of the dog's sight, again requiring a blind retrieve.

The Labrador, the Chesapeake Bay, and the golden are the best known retrievers.

During the past decade or two the retriever has been asked to flush game as well as to retrieve. This is strictly post-graduate work. The retriever is a specialist at his job, and should not be taught to flush game until he has mastered his primary function of retrieving birds. If the dog is allowed to hunt and flush game before he is fully trained to retrieve, the hunting desire and not the retrieving desire will dominate him, and with this diversity of interests, it will be hard to make a first class retriever of him. When a retriever is used for flushing game, he should work the same as a flushing dog and for the same reasons.

FLUSHING DOGS

A flushing dog's job is to find game by quartering 25 to 35 yards to the sides and forward of the hunter, to flush the game within shotgun range, to sit or "hup" to shot, and to mark the fall. The dog should also retrieve on command, after the hunter has reloaded. The springer spaniel is the best known of the flushing dogs. Only rarely does one encounter a cocker spaniel in the field today.

Once again, the dog who does not perform the task described is not completely trained. A flushing dog should be fully trained for the same reasons as a pointing dog. Hupping to shot is really the same as holding a point to shot. It fulfills the same function of not flushing the other birds before you can reload or frightening them from alighting nearby.

VERSATILE DOGS

Several fine breeds of hunting dogs have developed in Europe, many of them more versatile than the dogs originating in England. The European versatile dogs are generally divided into three groups according to their coats. The shorthaired group consists of the German shorthaired pointer,

1. The springer spaniel is a fine little versatile dog that can hunt a variety of game, including bobwhites, but ringnecks are his real forte.

the weimaraner, and the vizsla. The wirehaired group consists mainly of the German wirehaired pointer, the griffon, and the pudel-pointer. Of the long-haired group, the Brittany spaniel is the only member popular in North America.

The versatile dogs point like the English pointer and setter, but also have high retrieving and tracking instincts as well as an inborn love for water. They cannot be counted upon to perform in the field or in the water like specialists, but they do put in very fine performances in both areas. It's hard to expect a dog to have the hardiness of a Labrador or a Chesapeake for cold water retrieving in the late season, and at the same time be able to run all day through fields and woodlots hunting upland game birds in the warm weather of early fall. Generally, these dogs range closer to the gun than English setters and pointers, and because of their trailing abilities, are good retrievers of wounded game birds. Because of the creditable job they do in all phases of hunting, they have become quite popular with hunters who hunt both upland and wetland game.

Until recently, the main problem with the versatile dogs has been that there were no field trials designed to test their abilities. Trials for bird dogs do not require that a bird be retrieved from land, let alone from water. Consequently many versatile dogs have, over several generations, lost some of their retrieving abilities and fondness for water. German shorthairs that will not go into water and Brittanys that will not retrieve are all too common.

Field trials for versatile dogs, incorporating retrieving of game from land and water as well as trailing, are common in Europe, and have recently come to light in North America through their introduction by the North American Versatile Hunting Dog Association. The need for these trials on this continent is one of long standing.

HOUNDS

Everyone knows the merry little beagle. It is probably the most popular of all dogs. The beagle belongs to a category of hounds known as the trail hounds, probably the most widespread group of all hunting dogs. The basset, American foxhound, treeing Walker, black and tan, Plott, redbone, and bluetick are all trail hounds. Gaze hounds such as the greyhound, whippet, and Scottish deerhound are rarely used for hunting today.

The Walker, Trigg, July, and various other strains of American foxhounds were developed for fox hunting. The black and tan, the redbone, and the bluetick were developed as 'coon hounds, while the Plott was developed as a bear and wild boar hound. Most of these hounds can be trained to trail almost any kind of big game or varmints. The bigger hounds — the Plott, treeing Walker, redbone, bluetick, and black and tan — are generally used on cougar, bobcats, coons, foxes, and on deer in areas where it is legal, while the beagle and the basset are used on cottontails and occasionally on snowshoe hares. Beagles are also sometimes used for deer.

A well trained hound will trail only the game he has been taught to follow. For example, it is imperative that a 'coon hound run only coons. A hound that runs everything is worse than useless, and the hardest thing in training a hound is to get him to forget all the enticing smells he has come across that you don't want to hunt, like deer.

It is impossible to make a coonhound out of every hound. A foxhound will trail 'coons, but he does not have the "treeing" instinct. When the coon trees, the foxhound will bay a little and then run off looking for another coon to chase.

CHOOSING A DOG

Undoubtedly the best way to get yourself a good gun dog is to buy a puppy from proven parents. The proof can lie in what you have seen or in field trial records. It is unfortunate that in past years, at least in my opinion, field trials for pointing dogs run under the rules of the American Field, American Kennel Club, and the Canadian Kennel Club are no longer a guarantee of good hunting performance. The dogs in these trials generally range far too far from the handler to be of value for practical hunting, even in the so-called "shooting dog stakes". This is particularly true in thick cover. Retrieving is not required at most field trials; in fact, birds are rarely shot. My sentiments about this are shared by other experienced hunters. As far as bench shows go, a "hunting" dog can become a "champion" without ever having had a bird in its mouth.

Good field trials, with dependable results, are, however, run for retrievers, spaniels, hounds, and the versatile dogs.

The personal experience of hunting with at least one of the parents of your prospective choice in a dog is the best bet in choosing your new hunting companion. The second best is the personal knowledge of a hunting partner or some other reliable party. One thing that is good about field trials is that they are good places to see dogs in action. Interested parties are almost always welcome, gratis, and offspring of top field trial performers are usually for sale.

One decision that every potential dog owner must make is whether to buy a puppy or a mature, trained dog. I, personally, would never buy a mature dog. There are two sides to this coin. Puppies can be fun. Training a puppy is a mutually instructive experience. The very act of training a pup and raising it to maturity creates a closer bond between the dog and you. Even if you do not have the ability, patience, knowledge, time, or interest to train a pup, it is worth considering buying one and having it professionally trained.

On the other hand, you can tell more about a mature dog's disposition and abilities. A mature dog is long past puppyhood health hazards and it is ready to hunt, while it takes a puppy a year or more before he becomes an asset in the marsh or the uplands.

If you are thinking of buying a mature dog, remember that when a mature dog is offered for sale, there is usually a reason for it. It may be that the owner had hoped for a top field trial performer and the dog has not met these expectations or it could be that the dog is infertile, and thus useless as a brood bitch or stud. Such dogs make very fine hunting companions. However, be on the lookout for other reasons for the dog's being sold, such as lack of intelligence and hunting desire, gun shyness, or other undesirable characteristics such as fighting, incurable barking, or killing chickens and stock.

I would recommend that you never buy an older dog you have not seen in action. Have the owner show you how the dog performs on game. Try handling the dog yourself while the owner is with you. See how the dog reacts to guns and to shooting.

Anyone buying a mature hunting dog by mail should realize that he is gambling. If he is not satisfied he may be able to return the dog for refund, but he will still have to pay the shipping expenses. These may amount to as much as the price of the dog. If you ever buy a mail order dog on trial, be sure to ask specific questions about the dog's abilities and training and clearly state what you want. Demand positive written statements and save all correspondence including copies of your own letters so that you have the best legal case possible, just in case you need it.

As far as physical attributes are concerned, there are many things to consider in choosing a dog. Size can be important when purchasing a gun dog, particularly if you live in an apartment or any other place where space for the dog is restricted. Apartment dwellers will find that dogs under 22 inches are probably better choices, while people in suburban and rural areas should not encounter any great housing problems even with large breeds such as the Chesapeake Bay retriever.

Color and hair length may also be important. Some people are color conscious. Longhaired dogs collect burrs, but they generally clean them out themselves, and it takes only a minute with a comb to get any burrs the dog can't reach. Shorthaired dogs shed as much as longhaired dogs, but it doesn't seem to be quite as noticeable. Brushing the dog regularly, particularly in the spring and fall when old coats are shed and new ones grown, generally avoids much of the hair shedding problem.

Once you have selected the breed of dog you want, the next step is to carefully investigate the market. This can take several weeks or months.

Every gun dog breed has a club. All of these clubs publish a newsletter or a magazine on their breed, field trial results, and the club's past and future activities. These publications are excellent and reliable market sources. The addresses of the various clubs and information on specific breeds can be obtained through any of the following:

1. The American Kennel Club, 51 Madison Avenue, New York, New York 10010.

2. The Canadian Kennel Club, 111 Eglinton Avenue East, Toronto 12, Ontario.
3. The American Field, 222 West Adams Street, Chicago, Illinois 60606.
4. The North American Versatile Hunting Dog Association, Dr. E. D. Bailey, Secretary, R. R. 1, Puslinch, Ontario.
5. The United Kennel Club, Mr. Fred Miller, 321 W. Cedar St., Kalamazoo, Michigan 49006

You might also try the large daily newspapers and the general outdoor magazines for advertisements of puppies for sale. Correspondence with the advertisers of puppies will glean you something about the hunting abilities of the pup's parents, but beware of accepting the seller's word. Most sellers are "kennel blind". It is difficult for an owner to be objective about the abilities of his favorite hunting dog. A few sellers may even be unscrupulous. The ideal is to arrange with the seller to show you how the parents of the puppies perform in the field. Verify all statements about field trial wins with the field trial secretary of the club that sponsored the trial.

HOW TO BUY A PUPPY

Here are five tips for buying a puppy:

1. Only consider puppies who are registered with a recognized breed or kennel club. When you pay for the dog, insist upon the registration papers. If the breeder does not have them, hold 50% of the payment back until the papers arrive. You can remit the remainder upon receipt of the papers. This is the only way you can be reasonably certain of what you are getting. Investigate the reputation of the breeder if at all possible, and buy only from a known breeder who hunts or field trials his dog.

2. Make certain that the dam and sire of the pup have been used for hunting. Avoid buying a puppy from parents who are shown only on the bench and are not hunted.

3. Pick a puppy who is bold, alert, and merry, all qualities indicating good health. Avoid very shy dogs.

4. Obtain a health record for the puppy, including what inoculations the pup has been given and when it was last wormed. Your veterinarian will want this record to proceed with further inoculations.

5. Obtain a written guarantee from the breeder that if the puppy should develop hip dysplasia you will be given another puppy or your money will be refunded. Hip dysplasia can only be diagnosed by X-ray when the dog is mature. The disease is strictly hereditary, and a badly dysplastic dog cannot run for long. A hunting dog that cannot run is of little use.

Chapter III

Garb for the Game

The old adage that "clothes make the man" is certainly true in hunting. Clothes play an important part in making the hunter. No hunter can stay out long in cold or wet weather unless he is properly dressed. Hunting clothes even play an important role in the success or failure of the hunt. How? A hunter dressed in blaze orange is not likely to bag many ducks. A deer hunter dressed in stiff, scratchy — noisy — clothes decreases his chances of bagging a deer. A hunter who spends much of his time in camp because he did not bring along cold weather clothes or rain wear is not really hunting.

The less tangible things are also important. A deer hunter shivering on a deer stand loses much of his alertness and hampers his vigil. In short, he becomes less efficient. Being too hot can also be distracting. Finally clothes, or rather their color, serve a major function in hunting safety.

When choosing clothing, you must bear in mind the type of hunting you are most likely to do. The upland game bird hunter in the fall should choose cool clothing because of the likelihood of fairly warm weather and the amount of walking he has to do in a day. Duck hunters, on the other hand, do very little walking and warm clothes are usually desirable, particularly in adverse weather. The big game hunter is another story. Because he fluctuates between strenuous effort and rest, his clothing must provide a layer of insulation, a layer of absorption to deal with body perspiration, and some sort of shell to keep wind from getting through the insulation to his body.

Waterproofing keeps the water out, but in itself has no insulation for keeping heat against the body. Thus, rubber rain gear will be hot or cold depending on the outdoor temperature. Wet or damp clothing likewise becomes cold.

The hunter must always bear in mind when traveling by car and particularly by airplane that only a limited amount of gear can be taken along on a trip. The airlines generally allow 44 pounds of luggage, including rifle, per person. Small charter aircraft may be even more cramped for space. If you are going on a once-in-a-lifetime hunting trip a long distance from home, be sure to ask the outfitter or perhaps even the local inhabitants what type of clothing would be most useful in the particular area at that time of year.

Before you leave on your trip, make certain that all your clothing is comfortable and loose-fitting enough so as not to hamper your movements during the times you are physically active.

FOOTWEAR

Boots are the most critical item of hunting clothing. On many hunts, the hunter must walk unaccustomed distances, and without comfortable boots, his feet will soon be put out of commission.

For upland bird shooting in dry fall weather, light leather boots are the best. They should not be higher than 8 inches, and I would recommend boots made of leather treated with waterproofing, because fall mornings can be dewy and standing water is occasionally encountered in fields and forests. Nothing is more uncomfortable than wet boots. For hunting in the mountains, the boots should have grip-type Vibram soles for better traction on rocks. European hiking boots are another excellent choice.

For cold weather hunting, leather-topped rubber-bottomed pacs with felt liners are best. If you are going to be on snowshoes, moccasins are the best choice, but felt-lined "snowmobile boots" are also surprisingly good. For hunting in wet weather or for mild weather hunting in muskeg, rubber boots are the only thing that will keep your feet dry. For duck hunting in ponds and shallow marshes, hip waders or chest waders are a must.

The big game hunter will generally need two pairs of boots, the 8-inch leather boot equipped with the Vibram sole and the leather-topped, rubber-bottomed pac of similar height for use in rain, light snow, and muskeg.

All boots should be purchased about ½-size larger than the normal dress shoe and as light in weight as possible. It is far less tiring to lift light boots over many miles of walking than to lift heavy boots.

Nylon and cotton socks are fine for mild weather hunting, but light woolen socks are better. For cold weather, two pairs of light socks are better than one pair of heavy woolen socks. It is the layer of air between the socks that insulates the most.

PANTS, SHIRTS, AND UNDERWEAR

For upland bird gunning, so-called "bird shooter" pants of green cotton or denim and faced with sturdy canvas or nylon against thorns and briars are the best. Pants should be worn over boot tops, not inside boots, so that weed seeds an other debris do not fall into the boots.

For hunting in cold weather, particularly waterfowl hunting where the hunter is stationary, insulated canvas pants are a good bet. Some hunters prefer to wear a light pair of woolen pants with light canvas pants over the top. For big game hunting, woolen pants are best. The temperatures will dictate how thick and heavy these pants should be. It is wise to have a light and a heavy pair on every hunting trip.

Both cotton and wool shirts are popular for hunting, but in my opinion wool shirts are best. Again, their thickness and weight are dictated by the weather. It is better to have two lighter shirts than one heavy one.

Long underwear is generally recommended for the hunter for both comfort in cool weather and leg protection against brush, sudden rain, and the friction of horseback riding. Two pieces are preferable. The two-layered type is the best, and for very cold weather, underwear of the quilted type, insulated with down or one of the artificial fibers, is highly recommended. Light cotton underwear can be worn underneath the quilted underwear to keep the nylon fabric from coming into direct contact with the body. This combination will generally keep the hunter warm in subzero temperatures.

HUNTING JACKETS

There is a tremendous variety of hunting jackets available on the market today. These range from light bird shooting vests to eiderdown insulated jackets for subzero weather.

The denim jacket is fairly popular in the west and is quite good for walking or riding through snaggy brush, as it is virtually indestructible. A cotton shirt with a bird-shooter vest is a good choice for upland game gunning in the early fall. For deer hunting, wool is the only practical material that is truly quiet. For cold or rainy weather, the jacket should be of the parka type with a hood. For riding the big game ranges of British Columbia during late October, a down-filled jacket is recommended. One jacket that should always go along on any big game hunting trip is an entirely waterproof raincoat. This should be bought in a large enough size that it can be put over a hunting jacket.

A jacket should always have ample pockets for numerous small articles that a hunter carries with him. The color of the coat must conform to the hunting regulations of the area.

HEADWEAR AND GLOVES

Aside from the feet, the hands and fingers are the most vulnerable areas in cold weather. Knitted jersey gloves are fine for mid-fall hunting, but they soak up water like a sponge. A good pair of leather-fronted driving gloves lined with fur is better for colder temperatures. All gloves must be loose and flexible so that fingers can be maneuvered easily to work the action of the gun. In extremely cold weather, the down-filled gauntlet-type mitts are the best.

Head gear for early season bird shooting can be anything from a cap to a

10-gallon cowboy hat. The European Tyrolean hats are quite attractive. However, for cold weather, a well insulated woolen hat with good ear flaps is the only sensible headwear. Again, headwear must conform in color to the regulations of the area in which you are hunting.

On any hunting trip, aside from rain gear and heavy outer clothing, you should make certain that you have one complete change of clothes from underwear out. This is essential in case you run into a mishap such as falling into a creek or ripping your trousers while climbing a fence. Hanging your extra change of clothing in the fresh air while you are wearing the second will make you more pleasant to live with in hunting camps where laundry facilities are not good.

There is a tremendous selection of hunting clothing on the market today. Be very critical when you are selecting it. Above all, use common sense. Make certain that the clothing fits loosely, not only for maximum comfort, but also for insulation and for free and easy movement. Avoid stiff and bulky garments. Purchase your garments well ahead of your hunt and have any alterations made well in advance of your departure.

The color of hunting clothing depends on what and where you are hunting. Some areas require red, blaze orange, yellow, or white clothing for big game hunting. These colors are for the hunter's safety and are a good idea for all deer hunting. For waterfowl and varmint hunting, drab colors are, of course, a must.

My only other thought on hunting clothes is that they be clean and presentable. Hunting and hunters are being criticized by people on all sides. To help counteract this, hunters must improve their image. Clothes can help. Even if all you can afford to hunt in are old blue jeans and a work shirt, there is no reason why the jeans and shirt cannot be clean and mended. Slovenliness detracts from hunters and from hunting.

Chapter IV

Gear for the Game

No hunter can go afield with just a gun and a license. He must be properly equipped. Even the bird hunter needs a folding pocket knife and something in which to carry his shells. In waterfowling and big game hunting, proper equipment can mean the difference between bagging the game and not. Proper equipment can also spell the difference between a comfortable and enjoyable hunt and one where you wish you had stayed at home.

OPTICS

Binoculars are an absolute must for hunting trips into the mountains or plains, but they are useful for almost any big game hunting, even for white-tails in the Maine woods. A hunter who has a good pair of binoculars and knows how to use them will see more game. Animals that you would never see with the naked eye suddenly loom into the viewing field of your binoculars. In the forests of northern Canada, my hunting partners and I have shot more than one moose because we had binoculars for glassing distant lakeshores and beaver meadows.

Binoculars are a big help in evaluating trophies. And when you spot the animal you want, binoculars can help to evaluate the terrain for a successful stalk.

I even find binoculars handy for waterfowl hunting on big marshes, bays, and stubble fields. They let me spot feeding areas that birds may be using. They are helpful for identifying ducks at a distance and for teaching me the differences between wing beats and profiles or silhouettes of different species. Nearly all species have different wing beats, and pond ducks, sea ducks, diving ducks, and mergansers all have different profiles. And on those "blue bird" days when ducks aren't moving, binoculars help to entertain me by letting me watch birds and other wildlife found on marshes and shores.

If I ever had to choose between a good pair of binoculars and a good 'scope for my rifle on a hunt for mountain game, I would choose the binoculars every time. 'Scopes have not improved the killing ranges of our cartridges. They only allow us to shoot more accurately. There isn't a big game trophy in the world that I couldn't kill just with iron sights, but you must spot the animal before you can stalk and shoot it.

Binoculars should be of good quality. Cheap ones are difficult to focus, have lenses with poor definition, and are hard on the eyes. The best all around power is 7 × 35. Binoculars with magnifications higher than 9 × 35 are generally too difficult to hold steady for long periods and are usually too heavy and bulky.

The spotting 'scope is another essential piece of equipment for big game hunting in the mountains or plains. Once the animals are located, the spotting 'scope is used to evaluate them, to see if they are worth going after. A 'scope of 20-power is generally sufficient. Usually the outfitter has spotting 'scopes for his guides, but not always. If you are planning a trip after big game in the mountains, don't gamble. Bring a spotting 'scope. Your guide may drop his down the side of a mountain the day before you arrive. Certainly a hunter who plans to hunt the western mountains without the services of a guide must have a spotting 'scope.

KNIVES

Next to the firearm, a good knife is the most important piece of equipment a hunter can own. Don't skimp on a knife. Buy one of good quality. Stick to a well known brand or have a custom knife maker make one for you. There are a fair number of good knife makers plying their craft today. Custom knives cost $40 and up, while good production knives can be had from $15 to $45. A good knife, properly cared for, will last a lifetime — just like a good shotgun or rifle.

The selection of good knives for the hunter has never been better. Generally a 5-inch blade is ample for our biggest game, and a 4-inch blade is ample for most tasks. For smaller game and birds, a 3-inch blade is plenty. Knives can be sheath knives or folding knives. The only thing that matters is that they be comfortable in your hand. Long-bladed hunting knives are the sign of a greenhorn.

The hunter generally does not need a wide-bladed skinning knife because he doesn't do that much skinning. Nor does he need a fine-bladed knife for caping heads. But both knives are useful for the hunter who wants to be well equipped and prepared. If you are hunting wilderness big game on your own, you should have a caping knife. Every hunter should also have an oil stone with fine and medium sides and a tin of light honing oil.

AXES

An axe is a must for wilderness big game hunts. It can be used for a multitude of chores from pitching camp to chopping fire wood to dressing out and quartering a moose or elk. Certainly in field dressing an elk or moose, an axe or hatchet is needed to split the breast bone at least part of the way. I prefer a short axe — a 20-inch axe with a 2-pound, single bladed head — to a hatchet any day. A short, light axe will do anything that a hatchet will do, and better. Its only drawback is that it is not as easy to carry.

When not in use, the axe head should be covered with a leather sheath to protect the edge and prevent accidents.

When buying an axe, avoid those with painted handles. Paint can hide flaws in the handle. Hickory is the best axe handle wood, but other hardwoods can be good as well. A file and a coarse stone should accompany the axe for touching up the edge. A dull axe, like a dull knife, is useless.

SLEEPING BAGS

Every big game hunter should have a warm sleeping bag. The down-filled ones are the lightest and the best. They are the only bags suitable for temperatures below freezing. The sleeping bag should be equipped with a cotton liner for easy laundering. The bag should be complemented with a good quality air mattress. The new, all foam mattresses are even better than air mattresses, but they are too bulky for pack trips.

A warm and comfortable "bed" is not to be underrated. You can't put in a hard day of hunting day after day if you are not sleeping well and not getting a good night's rest. Bagging game or bagging a top trophy frequently means putting in a long hard day. I'm of the old-fashioned opinion that all good things should be earned, particularly top trophies.

CAMPING EQUIPMENT

Hunters who plan to hunt in wilderness without the services of an outfitter will need the full complement of camping gear — tents, stoves, lanterns, cooking utensils, axes and saws, and so on.

Be sure your tents are roomy. Nothing gets on people's nerves more than cramped tents in bad weather. The old-fashioned well tents are still an excellent choice even if they take more time to pitch. There are, however, many fine tents on the market today that are of good quality, are easy and fast to pitch, and are sturdy when erected. One of the very best is the schooner-shaped tent because it has no center poles. My wife and I have been using one for several years with great success.

Your tent should have a sewn-in ground floor, and mosquito screens on the door and window openings. Mosquitoes and blackflies can still be abundant during early big game seasons.

One tip about tents. Generally those advertised as 4-man tents will sleep 4 men, but not with all their hunting gear. A 4-man tent is really the minimum size for two hunters. A party of four hunters should have two tents for sleeping and one kitchen tent with a stove for cooking and eating.

Gasoline-type lanterns — the pump type — are one example of basic

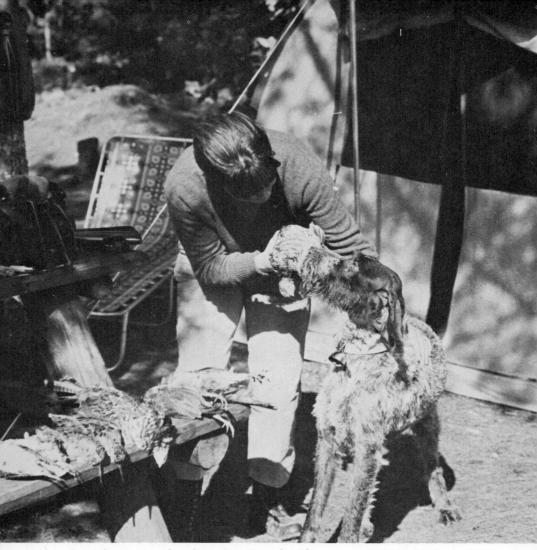

2. A hunter needs other equipment besides a gun. Everything from tents to packsacks are needed. This schooner tent has provided excellent service for the author on many hunting trips.

lighting for a tented camp. However, propane-type lanterns with rechargeable propane containers are becoming popular. They are somewhat more expensive to operate, but are cleaner and more convenient.

Most wilderness outfitters still use folding sheet iron cook stoves. Two-burner propane or gasoline stoves are a good choice for a couple of hunters. They are put into operation much more quickly when the hunter is in a hurry for a quick, warm lunch. Propane or gasoline tent heaters are also a worthwhile piece of equipment.

Cooking equipment should be the type that nests for easy packing. Pots and pans, except the skillet, should be of light metal. Iron is still the best material for skillets. But iron skillets are not for backpackers. All dishes should be made of metal or plastic-like material.

A Swede saw is usually better for cutting wood than an axe. Be sure to bring extra tent pegs and extra rope. Both may come in handy.

Unfortunately, I don't have the space to go into detail on how to choose camping equipment. If you are not certain what to buy, get a good book or two on camping and follow their advice.

One piece of gear that many hunters rarely think about are containers for clothing, hunting and camping gear, and food. Wooden boxes are the best for camping gear and food. Most professional outfitters and hunters who hunt regularly in wilderness areas with pack horses have special boxes made. Duffel bags, the kind with zippers across the top, are best for clothing and personal articles. They can easily be lashed to the back of a pack horse.

SURVIVAL EQUIPMENT

No big game hunter should go into the bush on a do-it-yourself hunt without a map of the area, a good reliable compass, and knowledge of how to use both. Survival may depend upon the compass. He should also have a waterproof container with matches. A pocket survival kit with flare signals, fishhooks, lures and line, snare wire, and a small candle or two is another wise piece of equipment. So are candy bars and survival rations. All of these can be safely tucked into the pocket of a hunting jacket. It can mean the difference between life and death, or at the very least it can mean being comfortable and well fed even when lost.

BOATS AND CANOES

For duck hunting on big waters, a boat may be as important as a gun. Also, in many areas of Canada, boats or canoes are used to get into big game country and even to hunt. Specialized duck hunting boats such as the "scull boat" are still made for the specialized methods of hunting ducks. A light car-top boat with a motor of medium horsepower is a good choice for getting into blinds or shooting areas on smaller lakes and marshes. For shooting diving ducks on large bodies of rough water, a 14 or even better a 16-foot boat with a good-sized motor is needed.

The canoe is generally used in wilderness areas and on small streams. Jump shooting ducks by floating a canoe down a lazy wooded stream is one of my favorite sports. A 16-foot canoe is a good length, but a 12 or 14-footer may be better on small creeks and beaver ponds. The shooting is done only by the man in the bow. The shooter and paddler take turns. One of the best ways to hunt moose in northern Manitoba, Ontario, and Quebec

3. Canoes and boats are frequently needed for hunting waterfowl, and in northern Canada they are useful for hunting big game.

is to paddle a canoe along the shorelines of lakes. During the early season moose feed heavily on aquatic vegetation. The shorelines are frequently the only bits of open country where a hunter can get a shot. Hunters can cover a much bigger area and do it far more quietly in a canoe. For moose hunting, a 16-foot canoe is the minimum recommended length, and an 18-footer is even better because of its larger load capacity. A moose, even when skinned out and quartered, is a heavy load.

It is almost not necessary to say that boats and canoes used for hunting should be painted dull colors. It is a good idea to have some camouflage netting draped over a canoe when jump shooting ducks or when using a boat as a floating blind. Life preservers and an extra paddle or oars are also mandatory pieces of equipment.

DECOYS AND CALLS

Old-fashioned wooden decoys are hard to beat. They are tough and ride the water more realistically than any others. Unfortunately even hollow wooden decoys are heavy, and all wooden decoys are expensive. It takes a fair amount of time to carve a fine wooden decoy from a block of cedar or pine. If you hunt ducks regularly and out of a boat, wooden decoys are your best bet. Because they last a long time — three generations if you take care of them — they are cheapest in the long run.

Plastic decoys have become very popular today. Their quality has certainly improved and they are now more rugged as well. For the casual duck hunter, they are fine. They are ideal for beaver pond or pothole shooting where they have to be carried a long way. Plastic goose decoys are very good for stubble shooting, as good as wood, and much lighter to carry.

Inflatable and rubber decoys are also available. These are useful only because of their portability. You can carry a dozen of these decoys in your hunting jacket pocket. Silhouette decoys of cardboard or plywood are fine for stubble shooting for both ducks and geese. They generally fold up and take very little storage room. Cork decoys are generally homemade. More recently, styrofoam decoys have appeared on the market. Styrofoam goose decoys are used for shooting on stubble fields or mud flats and can be disassembled and stacked. Floating decoys are also available in styrofoam. They are light and inexpensive, but very fragile. They are fine for shooting on stubble, but they ride poorly in water. All decoys used on water should be equipped with a lead anchor and dull green anchor cord long enough to reach the bottom.

Decoys are also used for crow shooting — both crow decoys and great horned owl decoys. These are generally made of plastic or papier-mâché. Plastic ones are generally better because they can withstand getting wet in a sudden shower.

For shooting pond ducks, a dozen decoys are enough. However, five dozen is not too big a stool for two hunters after diving ducks. For goose hunting on stubble, at least a dozen decoys are needed. For crow shooting, one owl decoy and half a dozen crows are enough.

Every duck hunter will accumulate a variety of calls, some of which will work for him and others that will not. Choosing a call is difficult. It works only by trial and error. No duck hunter worth his salt can resist buying or trying new calls — different brands and different types — with the hope of finding the "perfect" call. It's lots of fun. The same goes for goose calls, predator calls, crow calls, and elk whistles. Birch bark horns for calling moose are generally made on the spot. I had one on top of my gun cabinet — a gift from a Cree Indian guide — until in a moment of generosity I gave it away. It made a great conversation piece, even if I didn't know how to use it.

GUN CASES

Every fine firearm deserves the protection of a sturdy gun case. A good selection is available on the market, and can generally be divided into hard cases and soft cases. Hard cases are generally the luggage type. At one time they were made of oak, lined on the outside with fine leather and on the inside with velvet. Such cases can still be purchased, and fine English shotguns come with them.

Most hard cases today are made of plastic and lined with foam. They are sturdy and sell for a fraction of what the leather and oak cases cost. These hard cases can be obtained to fit entire rifles or disassembled shotguns. The hard case is a must for air travel, and for this purpose should be both light and sturdy. Guns packed in such cases can be shipped as baggage if you cannot get the captain to take them into the cockpit. In our era of airplane hijacking, a gun packed in a luggage case does not seem to raise any alarm. My only criticism of these cases is that most have flimsy locks. A light chain and padlock strung around the case and through the handle can solve the problem, but this should not be necessary. The cases should be equipped with better locks.

Soft gun cases can be made of canvas, leather, or plastic, the latter being the most common today. They are generally padded with some soft material. They are made in various lengths and styles for shotguns and 'scoped rifles. Soft cases are fine for automobile travel or where the gun is unlikely to receive any blows or be dropped. They should not be used for shipment by public carriers, at least not if you value your gun. If the lining in these cases, including the leather, fleece-lined ones, gets wet, it will cause rusting on the gun. In some gun cases the lining seems to absorb moisture from the air; therefore, it is not advisable to store guns in cases for prolonged periods.

The scabbard is a must for packing a rifle on a horseback hunt. The scabbard should be long enough to enclose most of the rifle stock, and wide enough to accommodate a 'scope if the rifle has one. Scabbards that are split back for about 5 inches at the open end will allow you to reach in quickly and grab the rifle as you jump off your horse. Any scabbard should have two strong straps about 40 inches long to secure it to the saddle.

A simple leather scabbard for a short, iron sighted carbine can be had for about $20. A full-length leather scabbard for a 'scope-sighted rifle will cost from $50 to $100 or more, depending on the quality of the leather and the workmanship.

CLEANING EQUIPMENT

For rifles, a one-piece steel rod covered with celluloid is by far the best bet for cleaning. However, such rods cannot be readily transported. For hunting trips, ideal rods are 2- or 3-piece takedowns of celluloid-covered steel. The one-piece rods should be used for heavy duty cleaning at home on the work bench. These rods should have a variety of brushes and jags in various calibres. The best cleaning rods are made by Parker Hale of Britain. Avoid all the little inexpensive cleaning kits with rods made of aluminum. They look good, but they will not stand up to long use nor are they strong enough to dislodge anything in the bore.

For a shotgun, a 3-piece wooden cleaning rod with various brushes and jags is hard to beat. Pull-throughs are fine for light cleaning, but if something is lodged in the barrel, only a stiff cleaning rod will get it out.

There are a number of fine gun oils available today. Some of the oils in aerosol spray cans are excellent. There are also some good pastes for stocks. Hoppes No. 9 is still a fine solvent for cleaning bores. A silicone-treated cloth is invaluable for wiping guns. Flannel cleaning patches can be purchased in all sizes, but many of us prefer to cut our own from old pajamas.

OTHER EQUIPMENT

If you are a gun tinkerer, a set of gunsmithing tools in a small case is a handy thing for extended trips. A bird shooter's vest is a handy item for carrying shot shells in the field. For a duck blind, a canvas shoulder bag is useful for the same purpose. I view game carriers from which to hang birds a must. Rubberized game pockets in hunting jackets prevent game from cooling quickly, and in my book are an invention of the devil. Metal ammunition boxes from army surplus stores are good for carrying spare ammo in the car. A small, light flashlight is invaluable for getting to a deer stand or to a duck blind and getting back to camp in the late hours. But be sure to have a soft, roll-up case for your gun or you may get into trouble with the game warden.

A light packsack can be a useful piece of equipment for carrying a spotting 'scope, lunch, rope, light, short axes, and even an extra pair of socks in case your feet get wet, an extra shirt or sweater if it gets chilly, and a poncho if it starts to rain. The liver and heart of your quarry can also be brought back in this. A light pack frame is useful for carrying out pieces of a big game animal if horses can't get to it or if you are your own horse. A packsack is also useful for carrying duck decoys and ducks.

LAST ADVICE

The only other advice I can give, and perhaps it is the most important, is buy the best you can afford. I learned this the hard way. Well made equipment, even if it is initially expensive, will prove to be cheaper in the long run. Junk never lasts.

Chapter V

Planning the Hunt

A hunting trip should be an enjoyable and rewarding experience in the outdoors. The kill of an animal may be the climax of the experience or even an anticlimax. One of the secrets to an enjoyable hunt lies in planning.

The old cliché "it's never too early" comes close to the truth in planning a hunting trip. For a big game hunt into the mountains of Alaska or British Columbia, a year's planning and preparation may be barely adequate. Many of the top outfitters are generally booked at least a year in advance.

For a small game hunt, it is generally not essential to plan a year ahead, but half that long is probably not too early, particularly if you are hiring a guide. The top waterfowl guides in Louisiana and the woodcock and grouse guides of New Brunswick tend to be booked fairly early for the peak of the season.

HOW TO PLAN A HUNT

The first step in planning a hunt is to determine what you want to hunt. What species do you give the highest priority? Are you after record book heads or will you settle for any respectable trophy? Once you have answered these questions, you can start planning the hunt.

First, read the section of this book on the species you are after. In this section you will learn where the species is found — its range. Then look up the addresses of game departments in the states and provinces where the species is found and write to them inquiring about hunting regulations and a list of licensed guides and outfitters, plus any other information that the game department might have. All of this will help you plan in more detail.

Perhaps you can only afford a low budget, do-it-yourself hunt with no guide. An inspection of the regulations will eliminate the Yukon and the Northwest Territories because non-residents must have a guide for hunting big game. However, in Alaska you do not need a guide to hunt moose. By process of elimination, Alaska becomes the only place for your moose hunt. But had you wanted to go on a combination moose and sheep hunt, you would have had to change your plans by either stretching your budget or scrapping the idea. Why? Because to hunt sheep in Alaska, a non-resident must have a guide.

The next step in your moose hunt is to plan where to go in Alaska. The information you received from the game department may give you a few more locations. If it doesn't, write to them once again asking for areas with good moose hunting prospects, for areas with high hunter success rates. You will get an answer. It may take a bit of time, but if you begin planning the hunt early enough, you should encounter no problems.

The next thing you will need are topographical maps of the area in which you will be hunting. Once you have these, this portion of the planning is over. Assembling your equipment comes next, and this has been covered in another chapter.

The steps used in planning a moose hunt are hypothetical, but they apply equally well to planning a hunt for almost any game species. Once you have the hunting regulations, you know where you stand. For example, you may find that some areas are open only to residents, or that non-residents are limited to only a part of the hunting season. A number of little problems may crop up which you must solve by planning around them.

The next step in the plan is to get your hunting license or permit. Getting a big game license and tags in Canada, Alaska, or many of the other states is no problem. You can purchase one upon arrival. But if you are planning an antelope hunt in Wyoming, you must enter a draw and hope that your name is pulled. There is a limit to the number of big game permits issued in many states.

HOW TO GET A BIG GAME PERMIT

More and more states are adopting a quota system on the number of animals to be harvested by limiting the number of permits or licenses available. Frequently the permit-quota system is refined to the point where each wildlife management area or zone is allocated a specific number of permits.

In some states, permits are available on a first-come, first-served basis, while in others it is a draw basis with a well announced date for deadlines by which applications must be submitted.

Each state differs on how applications for permits should be processed and handled. Some request that payment be sent along with the application, while others do not want immediate payment. In some cases, payment has to be submitted in a specific way — by certified cheque, money order, and so on.

The important thing here is to read the instructions carefully and follow them to the letter. If you do, your chances of getting a permit are better. It is not uncommon for over 20 percent of the applications to be rejected because of late arrival.

Here are several key tips on how to go about getting your permit.

— Be sure that your full name, address, and zip or postal code appear on both your application and the back of your cheque or money order.

— Make sure you are using the proper application form (some states have more than one for different species) and that you have stated the proper unit, area, or hunt number on the application. Make sure you have filled in second and third choices if offered.

— In the case of draws, some states have established a priority system for previously unsuccessful applicants. Check your unsuccessful applications to see if you qualify for such priority.

— If you are applying for a "party permit", available in some states, check the rulings on priorities. Often priority applications cannot be made on party permits, and remember that the party must also apply for the same unit or area.

— Don't make the mistake of applying more than once for the same permit. In this day of computerized checking, the computer may throw out both applications if it comes across a duplicate, and in some states duplication of applications is serious enough to cause revocation of your hunting license.

— Above all, get that application in on time. Check to see whether the deadline is a postmark date or whether the application must be in the hands of the conservation department by a specific date. Sometimes the mails are a bit slow, so get your application out as soon as possible.

Now that you've decided where and what you're hunting and know how to get a permit, the next problem encountered is hiring a guide. Hunter success rate, of course, is generally much higher for hunters with guides than without. To maximize your chances of bagging a trophy, especially if you're going a long distance for the hunt, it is a wise idea to invest more money into the hunt and hire a guide. A guide is also mandatory for hunters who do not have the equipment or the experience necessary for a wilderness hunt on their own. So the next step is to hire a guide.

HOW TO HIRE A GUIDE

When I speak of a guide, I really mean an outfitter. The outfitter will have all the equipment necessary for your hunt — saddle horses, pack-string, tents, boats and decoys, and so on. He will also have a crew of good guides. Any good outfitter won't have bum guides — they would spoil his business.

Most hunting outfitters are highly competent hombres who will give you full value for your money and will bust a trace to see that you get a chance at some good trophies. Unfortunately there are a few bad eggs in every business, hence there are some bum outfitters. Here's how to make sure you get a good one.

51

In some states and provinces, outfitters and guides must be licensed to ply their trade. If a guide is licensed, there is better than a 50-50 chance that he is a straight arrow.

From a listing of licensed guides, select three or four and write to them. If the state or province you plan to hunt in doesn't have a list of guides, look in the back pages of the major outdoor magazines such as *Outdoor Life, Field and Stream,* and *Sports Afield.* Some guides generally advertise in these magazines.

In your letter, ask about the types of services offered by the outfitter, the facilities, the game — including abundance and trophy quality, costs, and don't hesitate to indicate your preferences. If you have any physical handicaps, inquire about the terrain to make sure that the hunt will not be too much for you. Ask about how much time is actually spent hunting. A 7-day hunt may mean one day in, one day out, and only 5 days of hunting. Ask how many hunters to a guide. One to one is best; two to one may be acceptable; more than two to one is not, except for upland bird hunting where you can have three or four hunters to a guide. Most important, ask for a list of references. Reliable outfitters are eager to supply a list of previous clients.

On the basis of the answers you receive, contact several of the references. Ask them to evaluate the outfitter's hunting area and his accommodation. Are his guides capable? Do they know the area and the game? If you like the answers the references have given, you can go ahead and book the hunt. The best agreement is by signed contract, but good, clear letters are fine. Keep all of the outfitter's correspondence and keep carbon copies of your correspondence with the outfitter.

The outfitter will want a deposit — 25 percent is usual, but if may go as high as 50 percent with some outfitters. When you've placed your deposit, you can be pretty certain that a place is being reserved for you. With some outfitters the deposit is forfeited if you cancel the hunt 30, 60, 90, or even more days before the commencement of the hunt if the outfitter cannot find a replacement for you. In many cases this is fair. The outfitter has a big investment and a short season. He probably needs close to a full outfit to make an adequate profit. (Nobody ever gets rich in outfitting.)

Be sure you understand the conditions under which you can get your money back. Investigate the possibilities of cancellation insurance with your travel agent.

There is one shortcut in choosing an outfitter, and that is to book a hunt through a booking agent. There are a number of agents who specialize in booking big game hunting trips and safaris. These people generally deal only with reliable outfitters. Booking a hunt through an agent costs no more than booking directly with the outfitter. It is the outfitter that pays the agent a commission.

THE NEGLECTED DETAILS

Few hunters remember to contact a taxidermist before their big game hunt to obtain prices, and even more important, to see samples of the man's work. Don't neglect this. Choose your taxidermist carefully. Some are fine craftsmen, and others couldn't stuff a suitcase let alone a fine trophy head.

Secondly, devote some thought to a hunting partner. A partner with a sour disposition, the griper, the bitcher, the jealous guy, or the guy who doesn't know that hunting is supposed to be a challenge, and that adversities such as weather and "bad luck" are part of the game, will poison a hunting trip. This kind of partner will certainly take much of the joy out of it.

If you are planning a do-it-yourself wilderness hunt, a good dependable hunting partner is a must. On wilderness hunts, a hunting partner may become your life insurance, and you his. There are just too many things that can go wrong, too many accidents that can happen.

There is nothing like a hunting partner whom you know. And I don't mean just on a casual basis, I mean a guy with whom you've made many shorter hunts and who has always come through. You need a partner who knows when to give and when to take, a partner who will rejoice in your good luck if you bag a top trophy just as you would rejoice in his.

Choose your partner as carefully as you choose your outfitter. A mistake in either one can make for a pretty sour hunt. Stability is one of the key characteristics I look for in a hunting partner. Dependability is another, and experience is the third. A partner's temperament is important. Is he a sportsman? Is he a quitter when the going gets rough or will he go on until the last wolf howls? Does he have a pleasant personality? Is he a heavy drinker? You may like two or three fingers of Old Coonhound before you hit the sleeping bag; I like two or three fingers of Grouse. But a drunk is a handicap on any hunting trip.

A partner who qualifies in all these vital respects and loves the outdoors adds to every hunting trip. There is no doubt in my mind that a hunting trip should be shared with someone to be fully enjoyed. Besides, you need witnesses to back up your "story" about the 347-yard shot on the Wyoming pronghorn whose head is mounted in your den.

Chapter VI

After the Shot

How many times have you heard that wild meat is tough and gamy? How many times have you eaten such meat? Too many, I'll bet. I know I have and it's always at someone else's house. In our family we know how to treat game from the time the shot is fired to the time the roast is carved on the dining room table. Wild meat doesn't have to be tough and gamy. It can be tender, sweet, and delicious. The choice is largely up to the hunter.

The first thing to recognize is that some game species have better flavored meat than other species. There is no way that a scoter bagged on the coast of Maine is going to taste as good as a grain-fattened mallard shot on the Canadian prairies. The diets of these birds determine that. Yet the scoter can be quite flavorful, but the cooking techniques will have to be different.

The second thing that determines the flavor of wild meat is the condition of the animal. A bull moose shot during the latter part of the rut or shortly after the rut is generally in poor condition. The fat that the bull put on in the summer has been burned up chasing cows and battling other bulls. The bull will be lean and sinewy, and the meat will not be at its best.

The third thing determining the flavor of meat is how the animal was killed. A gut-shot buck that has been chased all over the north woods will not be as fine eating as one that was killed with one shot while it was browsing unalarmed. Why? The gut-shot buck was under stress. His system was full of adrenalin, and there is no way his meat will be prime. If you gut-shot a steer and chased it for half a day, it would be gamy as well. The only way to prevent this is to become a good shot and to pass up all long shots.

However, the most important factor in making wild meat tasty and tender is what happens to it between the shot and the kitchen. This is the part that separates the outdoorsmen from everyone else. Basically, the faster the game cools after being shot, the better it will taste. This applies to all game, from moose to mallards. All game, and big game in particular, should be properly aged. Getting really tender wild meat depends on aging.

FIELD DRESSING BIG GAME

First, let me shatter a myth that keeps persisting. You do not need to cut the throat of a big game animal to bleed it. "Sticking" a deer, elk, or moose to drain the blood from it is of little value once the heart has stopped beating. Your big game animal will be well enough bled if it is properly field dressed.

It is essential that big game animals be dressed immediately after shooting. Field dressing means opening and emptying the body cavity, thus allowing the animal to cool quickly. This is most easily accomplished by laying the animal on its back with its head uphill if possible. The animal may have to be anchored with rocks placed by its side or by spreading its legs apart and tying them to trees. When handling the animal, be certain not to touch the musk glands just below the hocks. These are marked by tufts of dark hair. The glands exude an oil which has a strong and unpleasant odor that can taint your hands. From your hands, the odor can be transferred to the meat.

The first step in field dressing is to loosen the anus and rectum by cutting around them in the rump, and to firmly tie them with a stout cord. A cut is then made in the skin and the abdominal wall from the pelvic bone right up to the rib cage. Cut slowly, with the edge of the knife pointing upward, working the blade between two fingers and lifting the skin and the abdominal wall away from the internal organs as you cut. Make sure you don't puncture the intestines. Cut around the penis and loosen it at this time.

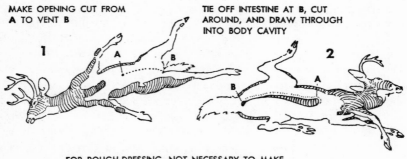

MAKE OPENING CUT FROM
A TO VENT B

TIE OFF INTESTINE AT B, CUT
AROUND, AND DRAW THROUGH
INTO BODY CAVITY

1

2

FOR ROUGH-DRESSING, NOT NECESSARY TO MAKE
ANY OTHER CUTS THAN THE ONE SHOWN ABOVE

Next, loosen the diaphragm, the wall of tissue separating the stomach and intestines from the lung and heart, by cutting around it close to the ribs. In deer-sized animals, you can now reach up and grab the windpipe and gullet. With a knife in your other hand, reach in and cut the windpipe and gullet off as high as possible. In elk and moose-sized animals, you will have to split the ribs with an axe or hatchet to reach the windpipe and gullet. When these have been freed, you can strip all the viscera and organs from the animal with a strong backward pull on the gullet and windpipe. An occasional cut with a knife may be necessary to help in freeing the internal organs from the mesentery tissues attaching them to the back of the animal. When you come to the pelvis, finish loosening the rectum by cutting from the inside of the carcass and pulling the anus through. Then drag the offal away from the carcass, keeping the heart and liver. This basic dressing technique works on all big game animals.

The next step is to clean up any spilled matter from the intestines and any blood from the inside of the carcass. A dry rag is best for this, but moss, leaves, or grass can be used. If you have to wash something off with water, dry the water away thoroughly. Meat that is left wet for any length of time can spoil.

You must also cut away the musk glands on the hind legs. With finger and thumb, pinch and pull up the glands while sliding a sharp knife under them and cutting right along the base. Throw the removed glands away and wash or wipe your hands and the knife carefully before touching any meat. Some hunters prefer to deal with the glands first, even before dressing the animal. This is fine if you are near water and can wash afterwards, but if you are far away from water, it is better not to take the chance of tainting your hands or knife.

When dealing with a trophy moose or elk, you cannot cut too far up the rib cage or you will ruin the cape for mounting. In such cases you should first get out all of the intestinal organs from the lungs backwards. Then skin out the cape. To do this, roll the animal on its side and make a cut on the back of the neck from behind the shoulders right up to within a couple of inches of the antlers. Now cut the skin around the chest through the middle of the shoulder blade on both sides. Carefully skin out the cape up to the last vertebra between the head and the neck. Sever the head, leaving it either to skin out later or for your taxidermist to skin out. You can now split the rib cage and remove the gullet and windpipe.

In early fall when the weather is very mild, it is frequently necessary to quarter a moose or elk carcass to get it cooled quickly. A field-dressed moose is still a massive animal. The meat on the animal's back is insulated from cool air by its hide and by the ground or snow on which it is lying. This meat can sour quickly. The best way to prevent this is to quarter the animal and hang it. Certainly if you want the best quality meat possible, you must skin and quarter every big game animal while it is still warm. Then place the meat in loose cheesecloth.

It is not always possible to skin out big game animals after every hunt. However, all big game should be kept off the ground after field dressing so that it can cool quickly. With elk or moose, you can prop up the carcass with logs or poles, or, of course, quarter and hang it. Deer-sized animals are usually hung whole, but even here skinning and quartering will improve the meat. The carcass should be left hanging in a cool, breezy spot to age. Keep it away from the sun. The length of the hanging period depends

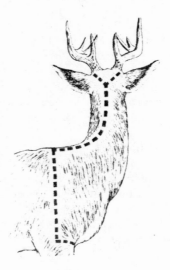

upon temperature. If the temperature is much above 50°, a 4 or 5 day hanging period is about right. If the temperature fluctuates between 25 and 40, 2 weeks is excellent. Beef is best when aged in a cold locker at 35° for 2 to 3 weeks. Likewise, the best place to age wild meat is in a meat locker where the temperature is kept at a constant 35°. The aging of wild meat is even more important than the aging of beef for tenderness. After aging, the meat is ready for cutting and wrapping for the freezer. You can have your butcher do this, or you can do it yourself. I, personally, prefer to do it myself. It's not a difficult task. Deer, moose, and elk can be cut up just like a steer. It's wise to trim away as much fat as possible.

A few words of warning are in order. In areas where deer hunting is good and popular, there are commercial meat packing houses that cut and wrap deer as a business. They usually have several hundred deer carcasses to deal with in a short time, thus there is no time to age the deer. The deer are cut and wrapped as quickly as possible. Your chances of getting *your* deer — the one you killed with a single, well placed shot and then field dressed and cared for very carefully — are slim. You may find that the deer you take home for your freezer was shot through the hind quarter and left an hour in the hot sun before it was field dressed. My advice? Stay away from these packing houses. Your first meal will show you that it was worth the extra trouble to deal with the animal personally.

SKINNING BIG GAME

Skinning big game animals such as deer, moose, and sheep is not difficult.

Generally the legs are cut off below the knee and hock joints. The skin is
then girdled and peeled away. The body can be skinned out very quickly.
In the case of bears, make the cuts as shown in the diagram. The feet are

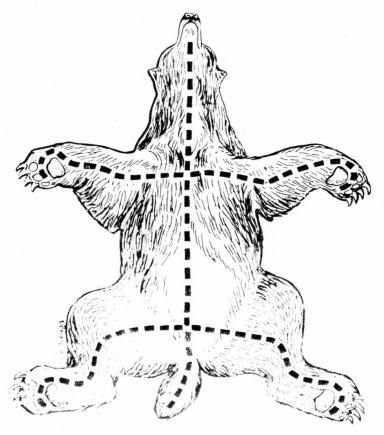

skinned out, keeping the claws on the foot if a rug is to be made from the
skin. The hoofs of mountain goats should also be left attached if a rug is
to be made.

Wolves, coyotes, and foxes are generally skinned or "cased". The pelt
then resembles a case or an envelope, without any cuts on the belly or front
of the legs. All skinning is much easier when the carcass is warm, thus it
should be done as soon after the shot as possible. Try to keep the hair
away from the meat. The hair of the pronghorn can taint the meat a little.

The head is the trickiest part of skinning big game. This, of course, has to be done if the head is to be mounted. If you can have the head frozen or get it to a taxidermist within a few days, leave it for him to deal with. There is less chance of his making a mistake or a wrong cut. If you are going to be in the bush for a couple of weeks, you must skin out the head yourself or the hair will start to slip. If this is the case, make cuts as shown in the diagram. Skin slowly and carefully, particularly around the eyes and lips. Cut the ears off flush with the skull. Cut the entire snout off where the septum between the nostrils meets the skull. Scrape all flesh away from the hide and salt the hide well, rubbing in the salt.

EQUIPMENT FOR DRESSING BIG GAME

Besides a good knife and a honing stone, the big game hunter may also need a hatchet or light axe, a meat saw, cheesecloth meat bags, and ropes and pulleys to dress his animals and properly care for the meat. A light axe is needed to split the pelvis of a moose or elk. A meat saw is best for getting through bones and for quartering big game, but this also can be done with a light axe. Meat bags are needed to protect the animal from flies in warm weather. Ropes and pulleys are needed to get a moose or elk off the ground and out of the woods. The type of game you are after dictates the equipment you will need.

DRESSING SMALL GAME

Rabbits and squirrels are easiest to skin out when they are still warm. Squirrels, once they are cold, are much more difficult.

The easiest way to skin small game is to behead the animal and cut off its feet and tail. Then pinch the skin on the back and cut through it, making the cut from the root of the tail to the neck. Stick the fingers of one hand around the carcass, inside the skin, and pull the skin away with the other hand. This is as easy as pulling off a glove.

If you don't want to skin your rabbits and squirrels right after shooting, you should at least field dress them. A technique similar to that for deer is used by many hunters, but here is a better method. Hold the rabbit belly up and make a small longitudinal incision about two inches long through the skin and abdominal wall right above the pelvic bones. Be careful not to cut the intestines. Grasp the rabbit by the chest with one hand and squeeze. Then grasp the rabbit with the other hand immediately below the first hand and squeeze again. Continue moving in this manner down the rabbit. The lungs, stomach, and intestines will bulge low in the abdominal cavity. Now give the rabbit a sharp jerk downward and the insides will pop out on the ground. If you do it right, you shouldn't have a speck of blood on your hands. There's a knack involved in this method — a bit of a trick. But once you try it on three or four rabbits, you'll have it down pat.

GAME BIRDS

The diet of game birds greatly influences their taste and flavor. As I stated before, there's a big difference between a mallard and a merganser, or between a mallard feeding on wheat in a stubble field and a mallard in a marsh. However, just as in big game, the flavor of game birds depends upon how the birds are treated after the shot. The worst thing you can do to a game bird is to put it in an airtight rubberized game pocket at the back of your hunting jacket, particularly on a warm day. Birds are best carried on a game carrier on a belt or over the shoulder, allowing air to circulate around them as much as possible.

DRESSING GAME BIRDS

Field dressing game birds as soon as they are retrieved is a good idea. Again, this hastens the cooling procedure, and it also helps to keep fluids from the punctured viscera out of the body cavity. For best flavor, game birds such as sage and spruce grouse should be dressed immediately and their crops removed. It is also a good idea to do this with ducks that eat a great deal of animal matter. With other game birds it's not as important, unless the birds have been badly shot up. It is, however, still a good idea to do it right away with all game birds.

Field dressing a game bird is easy. First, cut yourself a bird gutting hook about the length and thickness of a pencil from a branch. The hook portion is made from an off-running branch. Then cut a small slit in the bird by its vent and insert the hook deep into the bird's body cavity. Twist it around three or four times and pull out the entrails. Some European folding hunting knives have a bird gutting hook on them — a great idea. Detailed cleaning is done later.

If you are near water, field dressing can be done better with your hands. It takes only a moment to wash your hands and continue the hunt.

Field-dressed birds can be left hanging in a cool, breezy place for several days without impairing their flavor. In Europe, where game birds figure prominently in the national cuisine, birds are always hung and aged for 2 to 3 weeks. Not long ago I read an article in a hotel management magazine on a test conducted by the magazine on pheasants. The pheasants were treated in four different ways before cooking: frozen when fresh; frozen after aging; unfrozen and fresh; and unfrozen and aged. The chef of the hotel did not know which birds were which so that he wouldn't be prejudiced in his cooking. Likewise, the taste panel of gourmets didn't know which birds were which. The taste panel pronounced the aged pheasants far superior in flavor and tenderness to the unaged birds. Freezing played only a very small role in reducing the table quality of the birds.

Refrigeration is needed only if the birds are to be kept a week or more in very warm weather before being eaten or frozen.

SKINNING GAME BIRDS

Some hunters prefer to skin their birds, mainly because it is easier than plucking. However, to purists, skinning game birds such as quail, ruffed grouse, pheasants, mallards, and canvasbacks is blasphemy. Skinning removes much of the fine flavor, particularly if the birds are to be roasted. Skinned birds also dry out more in cooking. Birds that have been skinned are better cooked in a sauce or gravy, or coated first.

Ducks such as goldeneyes, bluebills, and the sea ducks are better skinned. Skinning removes some of the fat and the strong flavor with it. Skinning upland game birds is very easy. Simply loosen the skin on the breast and start peeling. Skinning ducks is much more difficult. You have to pull and cut, pull and cut.

PLUCKING GAME BIRDS

Plucking game birds is a more time consuming chore, particularly if there are many pinfeathers. Pluck the feathers by taking "pinches" of feathers between the thumb and the first two fingers. Remember to pull with the grain — the direction in which the feathers lie — and not against the grain or you will tear the skin. Do not take pinches that are too big or you will also tear the skin. All game birds, both upland and wetland, can be plucked dry. The old-time waterfowlers will tell you that ducks and geese are easier to pluck after being scalded in 145-degree water for about 20 seconds. This is true. However, scalding waterfowl is worthwhile only if there are many birds to be plucked. Setting up a scalding tub is a chore. With the small waterfowl limits of today, it is simpler to pluck the birds dry. The best way to scald a duck is to hold it by its head and dunk it into a bucket of scalding water. Waterfowl have hair-like fuzz over their bodies. This is best removed by singeing with a candle. After plucking and dressing, the birds must be washed carefully and dried. They are then ready for the oven or the freezer.

Most game that has been shot cleanly and quickly and properly handled after the shot will outclass anything you can buy in the supermarket, particularly with today's poultry, beef, and pork, fed on antibiotics and commercial livestock feed designed to accelerate growth rate.

Cooking game is an art. A game dinner, fully complemented with side trimmings and fine wines, can be a feast indeed. If you have done your part after the shot has been fired and before the meat reaches the kitchen, the dinner should be a noble end to a good hunt.

Chapter VII

Upland Game Birds

I know of no greater joy than autumn days in the uplands behind an eager gun dog. The fields and forests are at their finest then. The flaming scarlets and vibrant yellows seem brighter in the Indian summer sun. And the crisp, frosty mornings are full of pungent odors from fallen leaves. The autumn is a special time for all hunters, but for upland game hunters it is extra special.

Upland game gunning reaches its epitome with a well trained dog. If you don't have a dog, get one. The dog will add a new dimension to this sport that you never knew existed.

THE RUFFED GROUSE *Bonasa umbellus*

The ruffed grouse is a strikingly attractive bird without being gaudy. Its head, back of the neck, and upper parts of the body are light chestnut brown spotted with buff, grey, white and black. The head is peaked with a crest. On each side of the neck there are tufts of long, broad black feathers which form the "ruff" that gives the bird its name. The wings are streaked with pale buff and rufous. The fan-shaped tail is brown or grey and has a broad subterminal band of black.

Both sexes look essentially similar. However, the ruff on the female is generally less well developed. Also, the subterminal band on the hen's tail is generally interrupted in the middle. The cock weighs 24 to 30 ounces, while the hen weighs 18 to 22 ounces.

Hunting Hints — The ruffed grouse is found from Newfoundland (where it was introduced about a decade or so ago) to Vancouver Island and from central Alaska to northern Colorado. In the east its south-north distribution extends from the hills of Georgia to the end of the tree line south of James Bay. The "partridge" as the bird is sometimes affectionately called has a split personality. In the more remote areas, it's almost a "fool hen". Hunting the bird in the wilderness offers little challenge. A sitting grouse is easy to hit.

The ruffed grouse, however, becomes sophisticated very quickly. In the south the bird has lost all its naiveté. It flushes — literally explodes — in a thunder of wings. The hunter needs nerves of steel and lightning-fast reflexes to get a shot off at a grouse as it hurls itself around trees and disappears in the thick cover.

Since grouse are numerous only in good habitat, it is wise to hunt only there. This axiom seems simple, yet many grouse hunters — the majority of them — don't follow its dictates. The ruffed grouse is a forest bird but deep, mature forests are not its favorite habitat. The bird prefers the edge cover near forest openings and young forests that are still in their early stages of growth. Plenty of saplings and brush make up key grouse habitat. The bird feeds on a variety of fruits, berries, grasses, and wild clover. The only way to find good grouse covers is to go out and look for them. That is the best advice I can give.

A good dog is a real asset in grouse hunting, and a bum dog is a curse. Pointing dogs are used most often on grouse, but they have to have a keen

4. The ruffed grouse is considered by many to be our finest game bird. Here, Herr Schmardt's Boy Yancey, a fine pheasant and quail dog, is holding his first grouse. His master, Al Gallagher, is a darned good "grouse" shot, both the flying kind and the kind bottled by the Scottish gentlemen.

nose so that they won't "bump" — accidentally flush — birds. They must be well trained and biddable. A poorly trained, uncontrollable dog is worse than useless. A good grouse gun should be light, open choked and loaded with an ounce of 7½'s.

The ruffed grouse is an outstanding table bird. It can be easily over-cooked and if that happens its delicate white flesh will be dry. Because the grouse is such a fine table bird, so widely distributed, so hard to bag, and is hunted at a time of year when our woodlands are splashed with flaming reds and vibrant yellows, it is regarded by many hunters as the king of up-land game birds.

Outstanding ruffed grouse gunning can be found in Maine, New Hampshire, Vermont, Michigan, Wisconsin, Minnesota, Washington, New Brunswick, Quebec, Ontario, Manitoba, and Saskatchewan.

THE BLUE GROUSE　　　　*Dendragapus obscurus*

The blue grouse is a large bird. The cocks will occasionally tip the scales at 3 pounds. The blue grouse is also more spectacularly colored than the spruce and ruffed grouse. The upper parts of the cock, including the head and neck, are dull greyish-black with transverse lines of bluish-grey. The under parts, including the breast, are pale blue-grey becoming lighter to-ward the back. The tail consists of 20 broad feathers, dusky brown in color with ash grey marblings. Each tail feather ends with a wide band of light grey. The hen is similar to the cock except smaller. Her crown, breast, and sides tend to be marked with a bit more brown.

Hunting Hints — The blue grouse has adapted quite well to man. It is true that in remote areas of its range the bird has little fear of man. It is not uncommon for a big game hunter to come upon this big grouse as it struts about unalarmed a few yards away. But in areas where man's activity is a common occurrence, the blue grouse is a very wary bird. It will flush noisily and fly with an erratic pattern around any trees with skill equal to that of the ruffed grouse. Indeed, its flight may even be faster as the bird hurls itself down a steep hillside.

The blue grouse, like the spruce and the ruffed grouse, is a woodland species. In the summer and fall, the bird inhabits mixed open forests. His range frequently overlaps that of the ruffed grouse, but in such situations the blue grouse shows a definite preference for the dry open spots such as old burns, cutovers, openings near roads, and natural mountain meadows. These are the areas where berries, wild fruits, green shoots, and buds are most plentiful. And this is where the birds should be hunted.

During the fall when the blue grouse is feeding on berries and wild fruits, it is a fine table bird. Many people find it comparable to the ruffed grouse. There is little doubt that the blue grouse is as fine a game bird as any shot-gunner could wish for. It is too bad that it is not more widely distributed.

The blue grouse is strictly a western bird. It is found from southern Alaska to Colorado. British Columbia, Washington, Oregon, and Montana all have fine blue grouse hunting.

THE SPRUCE GROUSE   *Canachites canadensis*

Like all members of the grouse family, the spruce grouse is a striking bird. The cock is dark with the head, neck, and shoulders being grey and barred with black. The chest is sooty with white margins. The wings and back are greyish-brown. The hen is lighter and more somber. Her wings and upper parts are brown with variations of dull yellow and black. The under parts are whitish with tinges of brown. The tail feathers of both sexes end with an orange-brown band.

Hunting Hints — Unfortunately, the spruce grouse is not one of our better game birds. Spruce and jack pine needles are the bird's major diet in the late fall and winter. The birds at this time are not particularly good to eat. However, in the early fall when the birds are still feeding mainly on fruit and berries, the spruce grouse, particularly the young of the year, can be quite palatable and even tasty.

The spruce grouse is a bird of the evergreen forests, particularly the vast spruce stands of the north. Its range extends from Labrador westward to central Alaska. Its southward range is New England, the upper peninsula of Michigan, and the forests of Idaho and Oregon.

The spruce grouse is generally a very unsophisticated bird. Indeed it is frequently called the "fool hen". It will sit along a forest trail curiously watching the hunter approach. If it does fly, it's only to the nearest convenient limb. Hence most sportsmen rarely ever bother with hunting the spruce grouse. However, meat hunters do and for this reason the fool hen is numerous only in wilderness areas where meat hunters seldom travel.

THE SHARP-TAILED GROUSE   *Pedioecentes phasianellus*

The sharptail is a handsome bird of about 2 pounds. It is characterized by a short, pointed tail — hence its name. The sexes are similar with their upper parts being yellowish-buff, heavily flecked with brownish black, dull chestnut, and grey. The northern races tend to be somewhat darker. The cocks have orange colored air sacs on each side of the neck which are hidden by feathers when not inflated.

Hunting Hints — Most sportsmen believe that the sharptailed grouse is a bird of the prairies. Indeed, they frequently misname it the prairie chicken. Few realize that the sharptail also lives in open woodlands, coniferous areas, large burns or cutovers, muskeg, and bogs; consequently the sharptail enjoys a wide distribution. It ranges from the Quebec shore of James Bay south to Lake Huron's Manitoulin Island west through northern Canada to central Alaska and south from the Mackenzie River valley to Colorado. The place to hunt sharptails is in semi-open country — grasslands interspersed with trees and shrubs. The best shooting generally is near the clumps of poplar and brush that the westerners call "bluffs".

The sharp-tailed grouse is a great game bird. It holds so well for pointing dogs that dozens of professional American bird dog trainers come to the Canadian prairies each summer to train their pupils before the start of the coming hunting and field trial season. As a flier the sharptail is strong and fast. If it lived in dense habitat such as the ruffed grouse, not many would ever be shot. Last but not least, the sharptailed grouse is fine fare for the table. The flavor of a sharptail split in two, doused with bacon drippings, and broiled over a bed of hardwood coals is hard to beat.

The Saskatchewan prairies offer the best sharptail gunning on the continent, but Manitoba, Alberta, North Dakota, and the sand hills of Nebraska are all good. Areas of Idaho, Washington, and British Columbia also have fine gunning for the Columbian race of sharptails.

THE SAGE GROUSE _Centrocercus urophasianus_

The sage grouse is a large spectacular bird. An adult cock will weigh as much as 8 pounds, while a hen will perhaps weigh 5 pounds. The color of the bird is predominantly ash grey which is variegated with black, brown, and whitish-yellow. The wing covers are streaked with a dirty white color, while the under parts are yellowish grey except for a black patch on the abdomen. The tail is an extremely striking characteristic of this bird. It is composed of about 20 long, narrow, pointed feathers which a courting cock spreads into a spectacular fan. The hen has a somewhat similar appearance. She has a white throat and a much shorter and narrower tail.

Hunting Hints — The sage grouse is not a particularly good game bird. Its plumage and size may make it rather spectacular, but it is not a swift flier, consequently it is quite easy to hit. As the name of the bird implies, the sage grouse lives among the sagebrush on the dry plains. The bird is totally dependent on sagebrush for its survival. Sagebrush leaves are the bird's main food. The bird also depends on sagebrush for nesting, roosting, and loafing cover. And because of the sagebrush diet, the sage grouse is not a flavorful table bird. However, what the sage grouse lacks as a game bird, it makes up as an interesting species of an environment that does not produce much variety in wildlife. The place to hunt this big grouse is in areas where sage is abundant.

The best sage grouse hunting is probably in Idaho, but Montana, Wyoming, Colorado, Utah, Nevada, California, and Washington all have short open seasons on this cock of the sagebrush plain.

THE PRAIRIE CHICKEN _Tympanuchus spp._

The prairie chicken is a medium-sized grouse with a heavily barred body and short rounded tail. There are three races of the birds: the Attwater's, the lesser, and the greater prairie chickens, with slight differences in size and coloration being the main distinguishing features. The most characteristic feature of the prairie chicken is the elongated feathers on the side of the neck called the pinnae. During the courtship display, the pinnae stand erect like two horns. Both sexes look very similar. The cock has a prominent air sac on its throat which it inflates during courtship. The prairie chicken is sometimes called the pinnated grouse. It should not be confused with the sharp-tailed grouse which is sometimes wrongly referred to as the prairie chicken.

Hunting Hints — Hunting prairie chickens is similar to hunting sharptails. Weedy draws and grasslands near grain fields are the best covers. Chickens are unpredictable. They hold well one day and flush wild the next. Generally the young birds of the season hold better than the old birds. All birds hold best during the early season when the cover is thick. As the birds gather into larger packs, each consisting of several coveys, they are inclined to flush wild. It seems to be the case of one bird getting edgy and flushing, with the rest following.

When prairie chickens flush, they cackle. But frequently they also cackle as they are running through tall grass. This tends to give them away.

Walking the birds up is the favorite hunting method. A good pointing dog is a real advantage in hunting prairie chickens; however, one of the better ways of hunting these prairie grouse, particularly for the hunter who has no dog, is to locate a field where the birds are feeding. Then take a stand at dawn or in the late afternoon as the birds fly from the surrounding countryside into the field to feed. It's a good idea to check out the flight paths first, before the season opens, to make sure that a good stand is chosen.

A good gun for prairie chickens is a light full choked 12 with 7½ shot. In the early season a modified choke might be a bit better, while No. 6 shot may be better than 7½'s in the late season.

Only six states have chicken seasons — Texas, Oklahoma, New Mexico, Kansas, Nebraska, and South Dakota. The seasons are generally short. Kansas is the best chicken hunting state with harvests as high as 70,000 birds per season. Nebraska and Texas are probably next best.

THE WILLOW PTARMIGAN   *Lagopus lagopus*

The ptarmigan are our most northerly grouse. One of the unique characteristics of all ptarmigan is their plumage which changes color with the tundra in summer, autumn, and winter. The most dramatic change occurs between the summer-autumn plumage and the winter plumage. In winter the willow ptarmigan is solid white except for its black tail feathers. In summer the male is reddish brown on his head, neck, breast, and back. The back is also barred with black. The outer wing feathers and abdomen are white.

In autumn the reddish brown becomes paler and the barring decidedly more pronounced.

The hen in her summer plumage is a mixture of tawny brown and grey. She is also more heavily barred and spotted with dusky markings than the male. The outer wing feathers and abdomen are white as on the cock, and the hen also becomes paler in autumn.

Hunting Hints — The habitat of the willow ptarmigan is the well vegetated tundra and other northern barrens. In some areas it shows a definite preference for willow-bordered stream bottoms. In the winter, willow ptarmigan have been known to move right down to the timber line, particularly at higher elevations. These are the areas in which the bird should be hunted.

In size the willow ptarmigan is somewhat smaller than the ruffed grouse. Size, however, does not determine the stature of a game bird. The red grouse of Scotland, often regarded as the world's finest game bird, is in fact the Scottish race of willow ptarmigans. On the Scottish moors the birds are driven over blinds called "butts" by a line of beaters. The birds are in full flight when they come over the butts, thereby providing elusive and sporting targets.

Unfortunately, across much of North America, the willow ptarmigan is out of reach for many sportsmen. But not in Newfoundland. In Canada's tenth province, the birds are shot in the more traditional method of walking up, or on occasion over pointing dogs. In Newfoundland, as in Scotland, the willow ptarmigan is the king of the upland game birds. The willow ptarmigan is also an important game bird in Alaska. The birds there are frequently shot while on the ground with a .22 rifle.

The willow ptarmigan is a "circumpolar" game bird, being found around the entire north pole. In North America it ranges from Newfoundland through northern Canada including the Northwest Territories and the Yukon to Alaska.

THE ROCK PTARMIGAN *Lagopus mutus*

In size the rock ptarmigan is slightly smaller than the willow ptarmigan. In appearance it is somewhat similar. During the winter the rock ptarmigan is white, with the exception of the tail feathers which are black, and a thin black eye stripe running from the corner of the bill past the eye. It is this eye stripe that distinguishes it from the willow ptarmigan. In summer the upper parts, except the tail and wings, are brownish-yellow, finely marked with black. The male has a white breast and abdomen as well as the outer feathers of the wing. The female usually has less white on the breast. In the autumn the birds become somewhat paler.

Hunting Hints — The rock ptarmigan is a true arctic dweller. His distribution runs from the Ungava and the northern-most tip of Ellesmere

69

Island across the Arctic to the Aleutian Islands off Alaska and south to the high alpine tundra of the southern British Columbia Rockies.

Those who have hunted the rock ptarmigan claim him to be equal to his cousin the willow ptarmigan as a game bird. This is no small compliment. It is unfortunate that the rock ptarmigan lives in a country that is generally uninhabited, consequently not many sportsmen have had the opportunity to hunt him. In general, the rock ptarmigan lives in the drier, rocky, less vegetated parts of the tundra.

THE WHITE-TAILED PTARMIGAN   *Lagopus leucurus*

The white-tailed ptarmigan is the smallest of the ptarmigans; indeed, it is the smallest member of the grouse family. Its average weight is about one pound. Like all ptarmigan, it changes the color of its plumage with the season to match the color of the high mountain tundra. In winter it is completely white, even its outer tail feathers. This is what distinguishes it from the other ptarmigan, whose outer tail feathers are black. The outer tail feathers of the white-tailed ptarmigan remain white all summer and thus again serve as a distinguishing mark. This, of course, is how the bird got its name.

In summer the bird is finely marked with greyish-brown, white, and black on its head, neck, back, and breast. The tail, most of the wings, and the lower parts of the breast and abdomen are white even in summer.

Hunting Hints — It is difficult to generalize about the behavior of the white-tailed ptarmigan when they are hunted. In a few areas where hardier souls regularly climb to the mountain tundras to hunt the birds, they may be extremely wary and flush wildly, but more often they will hold tightly and rely on their cryptic coloration for protection. They will flush almost from under foot and fly like a covey of large quail, their raucous cries and the thunder of their wings filling the air. In more remote areas the birds are very unafraid. They curiously stand about as man approaches them. Such birds, of course, offer no sport for the hunter.

The white-tailed ptarmigan is one of our least known and probably least hunted upland game birds. The reasons for this are understandable. The bird is an inhabitant of the high alpine tundra, consequently its range is restricted to the Rocky Mountain chain from Alaska and the Yukon down to Colorado and even New Mexico. In most cases the bird lives far from large human habitations. It is most commonly shot by big game hunters and a few trappers who venture into the mountains. Other than that, the white-tailed ptarmigan is largely underharvested.

THE RING-NECKED PHEASANT   *Phasianus colchicus*

There is no need to describe the pheasant. Almost everyone knows the gaudy, long-tailed cock and the drab colored hen.

Hunting Hints — The place to hunt pheasants is in weedy fields and overgrown ditches, fence rows, and small ravines. Corn fields are good if overgrown with weeds. Don't waste your time in clean fields. In the late season, cocks hide in the thickest cover imaginable — edges of marshes and wetlands and even small woodlots. Don't ignore these just because they aren't typical pheasant covers.

What makes the pheasant such a fine game bird, outside of his fine qualities on the table, is his ability to sulk and hide. It is amazing that a bird so brightly colored can be so well camouflaged at the same time. The bird will run, sulk and hide, taking full advantage of every piece of cover before taking to the wing. It flies only when pushed to the limit by man and dog. This is why without a good dog, pheasant hunting can be such a futile sport. This is one of the reasons why, in a "cocks only" season, the pheasant is

5. The ring-necked pheasant has made himself right at home on this continent. South Dakota is the best pheasant state, but Nebraska and Iowa also have fine ringneck hunting. Southern Alberta is top pheasant country as well.

difficult to overshoot. Once the bird learns how to outwit man and dog, he becomes very difficult to bag. But the real boon in preventing overhunting is that only a few cocks are needed to service the hens. The old English game keepers knew this for many decades and modern wildlife biologists have reaffirmed it. But unfortunately sportsmen do not fully appreciate this and far too frequently, fearing overshooting, press for shorter seasons.

The pheasant range on the continent stretches from northern New England to central California and from southern Saskatchewan to the Texas panhandle. South Dakota is undoubtedly the top pheasant state, but southern Alberta may perhaps be even better. Nebraska, Iowa, eastern Washington, and pockets of Idaho all have excellent pheasant hunting.

THE HUNGARIAN PARTRIDGE   *Perdix perdix*

The Hungarian partridge should actually be called the grey partridge, but because the first birds were imported from Hungary, the name has stuck. In appearance, the "hun" is a chunky grey-brown bird about 12 ounces in weight. The chest is grey and the males frequently have a chestnut abdominal patch. The upper parts are chestnut brown, as are the abdominal tail feathers. The color of the tail feathers is very conspicuous in flight.

Hunting Hints — It is the speed of the Hungarian partridge that contributes to making it such a fine game bird. The hun seldom has anything but air between it and the gun, and it makes good use of it. However, the hun is also a fine bird for pointing dogs. It holds well. As a runner it is not as fast as the pheasant, but trickier. The ringneck runs in a straight line, but a covey of huns will twist and circle until only dogs with the keenest noses can locate them. On the table the hun is not as big as the pheasant, but what he lacks in size he makes up for in flavor. Can anyone ask more of a game bird? I can't. It's my favorite.

The places to hunt huns are grain stubbles and weedy fence rows and fields near grain stubbles. The hun is a farmland game bird. Its distribution is a wide one. The bird is found from Prince Edward Island on Canada's Atlantic coast right across to the southern tip of Vancouver Island on the Pacific coast and south to Idaho and the Dakotas.

The wheat stubbles of Saskatchewan are the best hun country on the continent, but the wheat stubbles of Idaho come a close second. Eastern Washington and Oregon also have fine hun gunning as does Alberta. Huntable populations are also scattered in parts of Ontario, New York, Nova Scotia, Montana, and the Dakotas.

THE CHUKAR PARTRIDGE   *Alectoris graeca*

The chukar is slightly larger than the hun. Its upper parts are bluish grey, while the under parts, including the breast, are whitish. The throat and cheeks are white and margined with a band of brownish black. The flanks are white with bars of brownish black. The most eye pleasing color, however, is reserved for the beak, legs, and feet which are red. Indeed, in Europe the bird is known as the red-legged partridge.

Hunting Hints — The chukar has established a fast reputation as a game bird that is difficult to bag. The birds are fast on their wings and feet. They usually travel and feed in coveys. In good cover they hold well for a pointing dog, particularly in early fall, but good cover is not plentiful in chukar country. The chukar's usual way of eluding hunters is to run. Frequently a whole covey can be seen running far ahead of the hunters.

The birds prefer a rugged habitat of deep, steep-sided valleys and canyons. These areas are sparsely vegetated and are characterized by rocky outcroppings of talus slopes. Cheat grass, sagebrush, juniper, or greasewood is the predominant vegetation of the chukar range. In the fall the birds move to slightly lower elevations, sometimes even to the farms near the valley floor. This is where they should be hunted.

The gun for chukar hunting should be light because of the long, hard hiking involved in this sport. Since the birds tend to flush wildly, the gun must throw a good pattern at a relatively long range. A full choked weapon is a good bet, but there are times, particularly during the early season, when a modified choke would be better. Consequently a double is hard to beat. High base 7½'s are the most popular shot size, but no doubt some hunters prefer 6's.

Perhaps the great thing about the chukar is not just the mere fact that it is a fine, difficult-to-bag game bird, but that it lives in a barren habitat supporting little other game and certainly no other game birds. For this reason, we should be glad to have it.

The chukar's range is restricted to the dry, rocky hills and canyons along the Rocky Mountains. The bird is also found from southern British Columbia south to Arizona. It is also found on the island of Hawaii. Utah is the top chukar state but eastern Oregon and Washington are also good, as is the northern half of Nevada. California, Idaho, Wyoming, and British Columbia also have excellent chukar hunting in local pockets.

THE BOBWHITE QUAIL *Colinus virginianus*

The bobwhite is a handsome bird with a plump body, a stumpy dark tail, and curved wings. Its size approximates that of the woodcock. Its coloring is attractive without being showy. The bobwhite's upper parts are reddish brown and its flanks are striped. The bird has a small crest on the top of its head which it can erect. The sexes are similar in appearance, but the cock has a white stripe above its eye and a white throat patch framed with black. In the hen the throat patch is buff.

Hunting Hints — The bobwhite is the king of game birds below the Mason-Dixon line. And bobwhite hunting is, in many ways, the pinnacle

of game bird gunning. A covey rocketing out of a ragweed patch is a sight
for the heart of any shotgunning man. And to see a fine, fast brace of setters or pointers dash with class and fury through the fields in their quest for
a covey of bobwhites is a sight forever to be cherished. A point! That, gentlemen, is bobwhite hunting.

6. *The bobwhite quail rates along with the ruffed grouse as our top*
game bird. Its range extends from Massachusetts and Illinois south
to Florida and Texas. Pointers and bobwhites go together like bacon
and eggs.

The place to hunt this speedy little game bird is in weedy ditches and fence rows by grain, corn or soybean fields. Weedy fields are also productive. This is where the birds live. Don't waste your time on clean barren fields. When a covey has been flushed, the birds scatter. Mark the singles well. They hold especially well for a dog. A good gun for bobwhites should be light, open choked, and loaded with No. 8 shot.

The bobwhite has a wide distribution. The bird is found from southern New England to Texas and from southern Ontario to Florida. The bird has been artificially introduced as far west as British Columbia, but without much success. It is difficult to pick a top bobwhite hunting state, but certainly Florida, Georgia, and Texas must come near the top. Such states as Iowa, southern Illinois, and Maryland also have good quail hunting.

THE CALIFORNIA QUAIL   *Lophortyx californicus*

The California quail is about the size of a woodcock. In appearance it is brown and blue-grey on its upper parts. The abdomen has a "scaly" pattern with a small chestnut patch. The flanks have white streaks. The key recognizing characteristic, however, is a black, forward curved plume standing from the crown on the bird's head. Both sexes are quite similar, but the male has a black throat bordered with white and the female tends to have a less scaly abdomen.

Hunting Hints — Hunting the California quail is no different from hunting other upland game birds — you must hunt where they live. The favored habitat of California quail is tall shrubbery interspersed with open areas or grassy and weedy patches. Weedy fence rows, brushy ravines, and odd uncultivated corners are the places to look.

The California quail is a confirmed runner. In escaping man it prefers to use its feet rather than its wings. As long as there is good ground to cover, it will flush, frequently far beyond shotgun range, and scatter into singles. When the covey is broken up the single birds rely on their coloration for protection and freeze tight until the "all clear" signal is given by the older birds in the covey. It is this habit of holding tight that offers the hunter the best chance to hunt California quail, but a keen-nosed dog is needed to find the single birds who sit almost until stepped upon.

The California quail is a western bird, found from south central Idaho to the Pacific coast and from northern Baja California to southern British Columbia. Oregon and California have the best California quail gunning, but pockets of Washington and Idaho are also good.

THE MOUNTAIN QUAIL   *Oreortyx pictus*

The mountain quail is the largest of our quail. A mature cock may weigh three quarters of a pound. In appearance it may be confused with the California quail because it too has a plume from the crown of its head. How-

75

ever, the plume on the mountain quail's head is straight, while that of the California quail is curved forward. The mountain quail is colored olive brown on its upper parts and slate grey on its lower parts, including the breast. The flanks have gold white bars upon chestnut. The throat is also chestnut.

Hunting Hints — The mountain quail is game for those of stout limb and heart. Hunting the bird requires much walking over steep hillsides, which demands endurance of a high order. The preferred home of this bird is the lower slopes of the Pacific mountains. Its actual habitat in the United States is highly diversified ranging from chaparral thickets to humid hillsides. Where the birds live near farmland, they will feed on waste grains, including corn. However, weed seeds make up the bulk of their diet. The hunting activity for the mountain quail must center around dense roosting and loafing cover and feed such as mountain rye, timothy, and wild oats. Water is another absolute requirement. Generally speaking, these birds will not be far from water.

The mountain quail is a runner. A covey will run as long as there is cover. The key strategy is to approach the birds from above if possible, because the birds always run uphill, but once their normal avenue of escape is cut off, they will flush. The mountain quail is a highly prized game bird by many sportsmen in the west because bagging it is difficult.

The mountain quail is found from the northern corner of Baja California to Washington and eastward to Idaho. Northern California and southern Oregon are the best states to hunt this interesting game bird.

THE SCALED QUAIL   *Callipepla squamata*

The scaled quail, sometimes called the blue quail or simply the "cotton-top" is an attractive bird. Both sexes look very much alike with the females being only slightly duller in color. The bird's back and upper parts are pale slate or blue grey while the breast and under parts are pale brown. The feathers on the upper back, the breast, and the abdomen are edged with black, giving the bird a "scaled" appearance. The heads of both sexes have short brown crests tipped with white.

Hunting Hints — The scaled quail is found from central Texas and Arizona across to New Mexico and from southern Colorado south to central Mexico. It is a bird of arid, brushy areas. Thick stands of chaparral and mesquite with open spots are good scaled quail habitat. But such brush cover as scrub oak, greasewood, broomweed, and desert hackberry all make good scaled quail habitat. These are the areas to hunt the bird.

The scaled quail also needs water and any good cover close enough to water holes is a good bet for hunting these birds.

This quail is hard to hunt. It doesn't hold well for a dog and it prefers to run rather than to fly. Indeed, I suspect that a fair number of scaled quail are shot on the ground. This may not be as unsporting as it sounds. First, it is difficult to get within shotgun range of the birds as they scurry ahead. Second, the birds can run at better than 15 miles per hour. Many hunters claim that shooting at running scaled quail is not unlike shooting at running cottontails.

In grassy areas the birds tend to hold a bit better. There is no covey shooting with this species. Even if you can get a covey of "blues" to sit tight in a brush patch, they tend to fly out in singles or twos and threes.

Texas is probably the best state to hunt this species of quail. West of the Pecos River is probably the best area. However, southern Arizona and southern New Mexico have local pockets with fine scaled quail gunning.

A good bobwhite gun is also a good choice for scaled quail. The birds are about the size of bobwhites, perhaps a shade larger.

THE GAMBEL'S QUAIL *Lophortyx gambelii*

The overall coloring of the Gambel's quail is chestnut and blue. Both sexes are similar in appearance. The back is bluish grey, the breast is grey, and the belly is buff with a black patch. The flanks are chestnut streaked with white. A conspicuous white stripe curves around the sides of the head and throat of the bird.

A curved top-knot or crest sits on the crown of both sexes as on the California quail. The Gambel's and the California quail actually look quite a bit alike. The black patch on the belly of the Gambel's quail is a good identifying mark. The California quail has a "scaled" belly.

Hunting Hints — The Gambel's quail is sometimes called the desert quail because it is found in the arid areas from southern Utah and California south to northern Mexico. It is also a difficult game bird to hunt because it prefers running to flying. Even in grassy areas, the birds do not hold really well for dogs on point; singles hold much better.

In the real desert habitat with its sparse vegetation, coveys of Gambel's quail will not hold at all. The only technique that seems to work is to try to break a covey up by running them down and then concentrate on the singles. This running down technique demands good physical condition on the part of the hunter. The desert quail country is hard on both man and dog. Heat and water shortages are continually present. Cacti and burrs are a menace to dogs. Even rattlesnakes can be a hazard.

Patches of hackberry are good Gambel's quail habitat. Hackberry provides not only cover, but food. The birds, however, eat a variety of seeds and wild fruits, including mesquite beans. Grains are also eaten in farming areas.

Good places to hunt Gambel's quail are near water tanks. This quail will always congregate near water. The cover around water holes and water courses is also a bit better. The southern desert areas of California are a

77

good bet for hunting this quail species. Arizona has even better Gambel's quail gunning, with one top spot being Marilopa county.

The Gambel's quail is a bit bigger than the bobwhite and has a reputation of being tough to kill. Because the gunning tends to be at long ranges, a modified or full choked shotgun is the best choice. The best shot size is 7½ but some gunners prefer No. 6.

THE MEARN'S QUAIL   *Cyrtonyx montezumae*

The Mearn's quail, or harlequin quail as many hunters know it, is well described by this latter name. Harlequin describes the face pattern of black and white with white stripes. The sides of the cock vary from slate grey to almost black with white spots. The upper parts are pale brown with black and reddish streaks along the back. The under parts are dark brown.

The female lacks the striking face pattern of the male. Her back and upper parts are mottled brown and barred with black. Her breast plumage is yellowish brown. The Mearn's quail is about the same size as the bobwhite, with an average weight of around 5 ounces.

Hunting Hints — The Mearn's quail is found from western Texas and southern New Mexico and Arizona to Central America. Although the bird is not as numerous as some of the other quail species, it is quite abundant in the grassy hills of eastern Sonora and northern Chihuahua of Mexico.

The harlequin will nearly always prefer to sit it out rather than fly or run. This makes him a fine game bird for pointing dogs. Indeed, pointing dogs are almost a must, because the dogless hunter will walk by many birds. The game dogs used for bobwhites will do a fine job on the harlequins.

In many areas the bird is unfamiliar with man and even in plain sight will refuse to fly or run. This has earned him the colloquial title of "fool quail."

The best places to hunt the Mearn's quail are grassy ridges and weedy fields. In very arid country, this quail will be found near water holes. Southern Arizona is probably the best area to hunt the Mearn's quail in the U.S., but hunters must know the local spots.

The same gun used for bobwhites is fine for Mearn's. It should be open choked and loaded with No. 8 shot.

THE WILD TURKEY   *Meleagris gallopavo*

In appearance the wild turkey is similar to the bronze domestic bird except that the tail feathers on the wild bird are tipped with brown instead of whitish or pale buff. The size of the wild bird varies with age and sex. Toms average about 14 pounds, hens about 9 pounds. The wild turkey is the largest upland game bird in North America.

Hunting Hints — Hunting is done by calling the toms in the spring. The hunter imitates the call of a tom, hoping to lure a rival gobbler within gun range. The call of a hen looking for a tom is also sometimes used. The principle in calling turkeys is the same as in calling the moose during the rut.

In the fall calling is also done. In this case the hunter locates a flock of turkeys and scatters them. He then hides and begins to call, like a lost lonely turkey. This is the call the birds use to regroup into a flock. Generally a 12 gauge full choke shotgun loaded with No. 4 shot is used for turkeys, but some hunters prefer a rifle like the .22 Winchester rimfire magnum where rifles can legally be used. The ordinary .22 rimfire is not adequate for big birds like turkeys and is generally illegal.

In an attempt to elude man — first the Indian with the bow and later the settler with the gun — the turkey has become an extremely shy and secretive bird. Many American hunters claim that bagging a big wise tom is more difficult than bagging a big wise whitetail buck. The turkey is a master of stealth and woodcraft.

> 7. *Wild turkey is the "big game" of upland bird hunting. Indeed, some states classify the turkey as big game with special permits and tags needed. Any hunter who can entice a gobbler within shotgun range in the spring deserves to bag him.*

There are several races of wild turkeys in North America. The most widely distributed and most numerous is the eastern wild turkey, but there is also Merriam's wild turkey, the Rio Grande wild turkey, the Florida wild turkey, and the Mexican wild turkey. All vary by somewhat different color variations in their plumage. The oscillated turkey found in Mexico's Yucatan Peninsula is a different species of bird altogether.

The wild turkey is found from Massachusetts to Florida and west through Texas to Colorado and Arizona and south to central Mexico. It is also found in scattered pockets of Manitoba to South Dakota and westward to Washington and California.

It is hard to pick the top turkey state, but the southern states have the longest seasons. Texas, Georgia, and Florida are all very good. But even such states as Pennsylvania have fine turkey hunting.

THE BAND-TAILED PIGEON *Columba fasciata*

In appearance the bandtail is a plump, robust looking bird, a little larger than the domestic pigeon. Its upper parts are brownish and purplish grey while the under parts are drab purplish. The sides of the neck have a glossy iridescence. There is also a white marking — a sort of collar — around the bird's neck at the nape. The squared tail has a prominent darkish band across its middle, dividing the tail into darker and lighter portions. It is this feature that gives the bird its name.

Hunting Hints — The bandtail is a very sporting bird. It is normally hunted by pass shooting as the birds fly through their flyways to and from roosting and feeding areas or during migration. The hunters take stands on ridges in a high pass between hills and shoot the birds as they fly by. The higher ridge tops are generally the best because the birds are more likely to be within effective shotgun range. Climbing to these high passes is a task for the hale and hardy.

The shooting is hard and fast. The birds, when in full flight, fly faster than a teal, and if there is a bit of wind, they slip and spin in the air currents with the agility of a snipe. A gunner with plenty of experience on high flying ducks will do better on bandtails than the average upland game hunter. The gun, like a duck gun, should be full choked, but it must be light to carry and fast swinging. The old bandtail shooters advise to lead the bird about twice as far as you would figure and then double it. Does anything more need to be said about the band-tailed pigeon as a sporting bird?

The bandtail nests in the coastal mountains from British Columbia to northern California and in the forested mountains of Utah, Colorado, Arizona, and New Mexico. It winters in the mountains of southern California, including Baja California, southern Arizona and New Mexico, the western corner of Texas, and southward through northern Mexico.

British Columbia, Washington, Oregon, and California offer the best

80

bandtail gunning, but local areas of Colorado, Utah, Arizona, and New Mexico are also good.

THE MOURNING DOVE *Zenaidura macroura*

In appearance the mourning dove resembles a slim, longtailed pigeon. It, of course, belongs to the pigeon family and could just as easily have been called the mourning pigeon. In several ways the mourning dove closely resembles the extinct passenger pigeon. Its coloration consists of subdued greyish brown with olive colored overtones on its upper parts and pinkish

8. *Mourning doves are our most widely hunted game birds. They are best hunted by taking a stand on the edge of a field in which the birds are feeding. The hunter should conceal himself by standing in shadows or behind brush.*

brown to buff on the under parts. When it flushes, its wings produce a twittering whistle, and during its extremely fast, twisting, rolling flight, the bird exposes white "flashes" on its outer tail feathers. Its voice is a slow plaintive "oh-woe-woe-woe" that is particularly noticeable in the spring.

Hunting Hints — The most popular dove hunting technique is for the hunters to take a stand behind some cover on the edge of a recently harvested grain field where doves are known to feed. It is wise to dress in dull colors. Doves can be almost as color conscious as ducks. The gunners should be placed in strategic positions to keep the birds moving and also to prevent most of the birds from slipping in and out of the field without offering a shot.

In the drier areas of the west, water holes are a big attraction for doves. The birds seem to choose one hole and water there in large numbers. The peak time for water hole shooting is late afternoon. Hunters should never take a stand too close to the water hole where the birds will become frightened and abandon the hole. Also, doves as they cup their wings to land are not very sporting targets.

It is wise never to shoot the same water hole or the same feeding field two days in succession so the birds won't abandon it. A 3-day rest period is even better.

Mourning doves can also be hunted by jump shooting. The hunter simply walks through fields where doves are feeding and shoots at birds that get up within shotgun range. Doves are wary birds, seldom letting the hunter get close.

Dove guns should have either full or modified chokes because the ranges tend to be on the long side. Generally 12 gauge is regarded as the best, but smaller gauges can be used. The best shot size is either 8's or 7½'s. A few dove hunters use 9's, while a few use 6's, but the smaller shot sizes are a little too light for the longer ranges and the 6's have too thin a pattern.

A retrieving dog is very useful. Downed doves can be difficult to find, particularly in corn fields where the corn stalks cover the ground.

The fast twisting flight makes mourning doves one of the hardest birds to hit. A score of one bird per 4 shots is probably better than average. Yet in spite of this, the mourning dove is the most popular game bird in terms of harvest. About 22 million birds are bagged each year. The fact that mourning doves still continue to expand their range northward into Canada and continue to increase in numbers is good evidence that hunting has no bearing on the abundance of game birds.

The breeding range of the mourning dove extends from Maine to British Columbia and from Ontario southward to central Mexico. Its wintering range extends from New Jersey in the east to California in the west and southward to Panama. There is excellent mourning dove gunning throughout the southern half of this continent. California, Texas, and Florida are probably the top mourning dove hunting states, but excellent mourning dove gunning can be had in many states.

WHITE-WINGED DOVE
Zenaida asiatica

The white-winged dove is a bird of the southwest. In appearance it is similar to the mourning dove, but the white-wing is slightly larger. Its overall coloring is brownish grey. The bird has a bluish black spot on the side of the head as well as a metallic bronze spot. The bird's tail is pointed. The whitewing gets its name from a large, white wing patch which is quite pronounced in flight. The female whitewing is slightly smaller than the male and is slightly duller in color.

Hunting Hints — The white-winged dove breeds from Texas and the southwest right to central Mexico and Baja California. It winters from northern Mexico south to Panama.

White-winged doves are hunted in a manner similar to mourning doves. Stubble fields are a favorite gunning place, but since the whitewing lives in rather dry areas, shooting near water holes is perhaps practiced more than with mourning doves. In some places pass shooting on whitewings can also be done.

No doubt the best places to gun the whitewing are in parts of Mexico including Baja California. In recent years many American hunters have discovered the fantastic whitewing hunting south of the border. The same type of gun and loads are used as for mourning doves. There is no difference in gunning for these two birds.

THE AMERICAN WOODCOCK
Philohela minor

The woodcock's general appearance is that of a compact brown, black and cinnamon ball with scarcely any tail and a rather long flexible bill. The bird's eyes are large, dark and very prominent. The rump, back and wings are black, russet and brown with the latter being the predominant color. These colors are blended into a "dead leaf pattern". The breast is cinnamon and the tail is black with grey tipping.

Hunting Hints — The woodcock's specialized habitat dictates where the bird should be hunted. You have to hunt woodcock where they feed and live. It is quite easy to find out if woodcock are using a particular woodlot — the bare earth will have small "drill holes", which the woodcock makes when probing for worms. Also the ground will have whitewash splotches of droppings about the size of a 25 cent piece. Both are unmistakable woodcock signs even if the birds are not there.

The woodcock's first line of defense is its dull coloration. The bird will crouch down hoping the danger will pass. Walk slowly, stopping every few steps, so that the bird becomes jittery and flushes. This technique should actually be used for all game birds. Most hunters walk too fast. The only

9. The woodcock, with its erratic, twisting flight, is a fine and tricky game bird to shoot. New Brunswick, Maine, Ontario, and Louisiana are the best places to hunt it.

time woodcock flush wildly is in windy weather.

The timberdoodle, as the woodcock is occasionally called, holds very well for dogs. And indeed woodcock hunting is most fun and most productive with a good pointing dog. The flushing dogs can also be used. The little cocker spaniel was bred especially for woodcock hunting, hence its name. Some dogs refuse to retrieve woodcock for unknown reasons.

Although woodcock are quite plentiful, because of their twisting erratic flight and the thick cover they inhabit, they are difficult targets to bag. A light open choked shotgun loaded with No. 7½ to 9 shot is ideal. The woodcock is a fine table bird, esteemed as a delicacy since the days of William Shakespeare.

Although woodcock are quite plentiful, they are not hunted a great deal. The average hunter is just not a woodcock fan. The birds are found from New Brunswick westward to Minnesota and even in scattered areas farther west. The main breeding range is east of the Mississippi with New Brunswick, Nova Scotia, Maine, Ontario, and Michigan being the top nesting areas. These are also the top gunning areas, along with Louisiana.

OTHER GAME BIRDS

The chachalaca *(Ortalis vetula)* is another game bird found in the United States, but only in a small corner of southern Texas thicket country. The chachalaca belongs to the same order (Galliformes) of birds as the quails and pheasants. It has a long green tail and a brown back. It usually lives in trees and bushes. It is an abundant and widely distributed game bird in Mexico. Indeed, Mexico has a number of upland game birds that are found nowhere else.

In some areas of the United States, the feral pigeon, more properly called the rock dove *(Columba livia)* is becoming something of a game bird. Feral pigeons are mostly associated with cities, but they nest in rocky canyons, under bridges, and in abandoned farm buildings. The feral pigeon is not protected by game laws because it is not recognized as a game bird. It offers difficult shotgunning and where it is hunted it is wary and difficult to approach within shotgun range. Gunning over a feeding area or a water hole is a better hunting technique. The feral pigeon can be eaten, but it is not nearly as good as the mourning dove. Pigeon breasts make very fine pigeon pot pie.

The Florida Keys also have the white-crowned pigeon *(Columba leuco-cephala)*, but this bird is protected in the United States. There are also a number of species of small doves and pigeons occurring in the southwest, southern California, and Florida, but none of these are hunted. None are particularly abundant.

The Iranian pheasant *(Phasianus cholchicus persicus)* has been recently introduced in West Virginia, but I doubt if it will ever become an important game bird.

Hawaii has a number of exotic game birds. The grey and black francolin *(Francolin spp.)*, partridge-like game birds of Africa, are two of them. I have not hunted francolins in Hawaii, but I have gunned for them in Africa. They are tremendous game birds, fast flying and good to eat. Hawaii also has Japanese quail *(Coturnix coturnix)*, but the bird is not particularly abundant. The Laceneck dove *(Streptopelia chinensis)* and the barred dove *(Geopelia striata)* are two other Hawaiian game birds. Both exist in fair numbers. Of course, all of the upland game birds in Hawaii are exotic to the islands. They have been introduced by man.

Upland game gunners on this continent have profited by the introduction of exotic game birds. The ring-necked pheasant, the Hungarian partridge, and the chukar are certainly valuable additions to our game list. The stocking of other exotic game birds has also been looked upon as a possible panacea for our game management problems, and many other game birds have been introduced to this continent without achieving anything. It has just been a colossal waste of time and money. There is no such thing as an easy

85

cure-all in upland game management. The time and money spent on this would have been better spent improving the habitat of native game species or exotic species which have already established themselves.

Chapter VIII

Waterfowl

A skein of geese honking in the sky will make even a city man look skyward. No other birds have this power, this attraction. Is it the tiny remnant of ancient times when all men were hunters and waterfowl meant food? Is it a manifestation of man's hunting instinct that the sophistry and sophistication of our jaded, and at times unreal society has not been able to completely eradicate, at least not yet anyway? Perhaps.

One thing, however, is certain. Without waterfowl, the hunting scene on this continent would be bleak indeed. Hunting wildfowl is a North American tradition of ancient lineage. It can be traced not only to the first European colonists but even back to the Indian hunters and their decoys of woven reeds.

Every wildfowler should be able to identify ducks and geese at a glance. Having such ability not only gives tremendous personal satisfaction but also makes every hunter a more knowledgeable outdoorsman. And there is another important reason for this knowledge. The sophisticated techniques of "species management" with its "point system" allowing birds of some species or sex to be harvested will work only if hunters can readily identify waterfowl on the wing. With some species of waterfowl being fully protected, it has become even more imperative that waterfowlers know their ducks and geese. There are a number of bird guides on the market that are good at teaching waterfowl identification. The pamphlet *Ducks at a Distance,* published by the U.S. Bureau of Sport Fisheries and Wildlife, available in the United States and in Canada through a courtesy arrangement with the Canadian Wildlife Service, is an excellent aid in learning to identify ducks. This pamphlet is available through federal government agencies in both Washington and Ottawa.

Ducks Unlimited (Canada), a sportsman's organization dedicated to the conservation of waterfowl also has an excellent waterfowl identification guide. Although it is free for the asking, $1 to cover postage and handling by this nonprofit organization would be, I am quite sure, most appreciated.

The pamphlet is available from Ducks Unlimited at 1495 Pembina Highway, Winnipeg, Manitoba, Canada R3T 2E2.

THE DABBLING DUCKS

The pond ducks as dabbling ducks are sometimes called, generally live in shallow marshes and rivers. They feed by "tipping up" to sift through the silt and vegetation on the bottom, not by diving or submerging completely under water. They can dive, but usually do so only to escape danger. Dabbling ducks can be identified by the small hind toe and by the way they spring up from the water during take-off. They are quite at home on land, and any ducks you see feeding in stubble fields will be the dabbling species.

THE MALLARD   *Anas platyrhynchos platyrhynchos*

Identification — The mallard or greenhead is our most common duck. The drake's reddish orange bill and green-purple head bordered by a white collar make him unmistakable. The female is mottled brown. Both sexes have metallic blue wing patches bordered with white. The average weight of a mallard is about two and a half pounds.

The mallard is the most numerous and widely distributed duck in North America. It breeds from western Quebec in the east to the British Columbia coast on the west, and from Alaska south to Utah and Colorado.

THE BLACK DUCK   *Anas rubripes*

Identification — Both sexes are mottled brown with lighter brown heads and have glossy purple wing patches bordered with black. The wing linings are white. The black duck weighs about two and a half pounds.

The black duck is an eastern duck. Its nesting range is limited from the southeastern corner of Manitoba to Newfoundland and from Labrador to Delaware. It winters from Massachusetts to Florida and west to Louisiana.

THE PINTAIL   *Anas acuta tzitzihoa*

Identification — The pintail is hard to mistake. The drake is a striking long-necked, long-tailed bird. It has a wing patch of metallic bronze-green. The hen has much more subdued coloring, with little or no green. She has no long tail feathers but her neck is quite slim and long. The wing linings are mottled dark grey-brown. The pintail is a fair-sized duck weighing about two pounds.

The pintail has a wide breeding range in the west. Its nesting area runs from the center of Hudson Bay to the Pacific coast and from northern Alaska to Utah and Colorado. The bird winters in the southeastern and southwestern United States as well as in Mexico.

10. *The pintail drake is one of our most beautiful dabbling ducks.
It breeds from Hudson Bay to the Pacific coast and from Alaska to
Utah, and winters from the southwestern to the southeastern states
and Mexico.*

THE TEALS
Anas spp.

Identification — There are three species of teal in North America. All of them are small fast flying ducks. The blue-winged teal is perhaps the best known. The drake is darkly colored with a white crest in front of its eye. It has prominent chalky blue shoulder patches, and a green speculum on the wings. The hen is dark brown in color and has the same chalky blue shoulder patch as the drake.

The green-winged teal is almost as well known as the bluewing. The drake greenwing is dark brown, with a vertical white bar separating the spotted, buff colored chest from the grey sides. The hen is mottled brown. As the name suggests, both sexes have considerable green on their wings; the speculum is metallic green.

The cinnamon teal is the least known of the teals. The drake has a distinctive overall dark cinnamon-red plumage. The female is mottled brown-buff in color. The hen cinnamon teal is virtually identical to the hen blue-wing. Both sexes of cinnamon teal have chalky blue wing patches identical to blue-winged teal. All teal are quite small, weighing about 12 ounces.

The breeding range of these birds is, however, different. The cinnamon teal breeds in the southern, mountainous areas of British Columbia and Alberta south to central Mexico and from central Colorado to the Pacific coast. The blue-winged teal breeds from eastern New York to British Columbia and Oregon, and from the southern part of the Yukon to central Colorado. The nesting area of the greenwing ranges from western Wisconsin to the Pacific coast in Canada, including parts of Washington, Oregon, and California, and from Alaska and the Mackenzie River Delta to Wyoming.

THE AMERICAN WIDGEON   *Mareca americana*

Identification — The American widgeon is sometimes better known as the baldpate. The drake is easy to identify by its white crown, dark mask through the eyes, bold white wing shoulder patches, and metallic green and black speculum. The hen is conspicuously brown, with grey head, greyish white shoulder patches, and a similar speculum to that of the drake but duller in color. The widgeon weighs about one and three quarter pounds.

The main breeding range of the widgeon is in the western part of North America from western Lake Superior to western Nevada, and from Alaska and the Mackenzie River Delta to central Colorado and northern Kansas. The bird winters along the Pacific and Atlantic coasts of the United States, including the gulf coast, and Mexico.

THE LESS NUMEROUS SPECIES

The gadwall *(Anas strepera)* and the shoveller *(Spatula clypeata)* are not as numerous as the other dabbling ducks. The gadwall drake is greyish colored with brown head and black chest. The hen is dull brown. Both sexes have a wing patch of white, black, and chestnut which makes them easy to identify. The average weight of the gadwall is about one and three quarter pounds.

The gadwall breeds on the prairies of Manitoba, Saskatchewan and Alberta and in the open country of central British Columbia, south to northern California in the west and western Iowa.

The shoveller is a colorful duck. The drake has a glossy green head, white chest, and chestnut red sides. The female is plain brown. Both sexes have strikingly blue colored shoulder wing patches. But it is the over-sized spoon-shaped bill that makes this duck unique. The shoveller weighs about one and one quarter pounds. It breeds from Lake Superior west to central California and from the Bering Sea to central Colorado.

The mottled duck *(Anas fulvigula)*, sometimes called the Florida duck, nests in the southern half of Florida and along the gulf coast from Mississippi to northern Mexico. In appearance the mottled duck is very similar to the black duck or the female mallard. It has a yellow bill which distinguishes it from the mallard, and has a white border behind the blue speculum on the wing. Both sexes are similar in appearance.

The New Mexican duck *(Anas diazi)* is unknown to most waterfowlers. This is not surprising, as the bird is found only in the Rio Grande River valley west to El Paso and north to Albuquerque, New Mexico. Both sexes of the New Mexican duck are difficult to distinguish from the female mallard. The female Mexican duck has an orange bill with a black nail, while the drake has a yellowish bill.

THE WOOD DUCK   *Aix sponsa*

Identification — The male wood duck is our most spectacularly colored duck. Its head has a striking crest. Rainbow hues of metallic green, blue, and bronze predominate on its head and wings. Its chin and throat are white. The hen is less colorful, with a mixture of grey-brown and green. The crest on her head is smaller than that of the drake. The wood duck is not large, weighing about one and a half pounds.

The wood duck's breeding range lies from south central Manitoba through New Brunswick and south to Florida and the gulf coast of Texas. Wood ducks also breed in south central Manitoba and in southern British Columbia including Vancouver Island.

THE TREE DUCKS   *Dendrocygna* spp.

Identification — Two species of tree ducks, the blackbellied and the Fulvous, are found in the United States. The name tree duck, however, is something of a misnomer as neither species nest in trees very often. They are both characterized by long necks and long legs, giving them a somewhat unducklike appearance.

The black-bellied tree duck *(Dendrocygna autumnalis)* has a striking black breast and belly. The underside of the wings are also dark. The outside of the wings have large white areas which are very conspicuous in flight. The legs and feet are pink. Both sexes look alike. The black-bellied tree duck weighs about one and a half pounds.

The Fulvous tree duck *(Dendrocygna bicolor)* has a belly, breast, and head of deep tawny yellow. The back and wings are dark, with both sexes looking alike. The Fulvous tree duck is about the same size as the black-bellied tree duck.

The black-bellied tree duck nests and winters from the southern tip of Texas through most of Mexico to Panama, while the Fulvous tree duck nests and winters from the gulf coast of Texas and southern California down to central Mexico.

91

HUNTING THE DABBLING DUCKS

Duck hunting to the average hunter means hunting mallards on some small marsh or perhaps black ducks on a lazy creek. Dabbling ducks, because they live on small waters, are more widely available to hunters than are diving ducks.

Knowing what wetland the dabbling ducks are using — for feeding, loafing, and roosting — is the key to successful pond duck hunting. The only way to find this out is through long duck hunting experience in the area or actually going out to scout an area before the season opens.

The next thing is to know how and where to set your decoys. Too many hunters dash into a clump of reeds and throw out their decoys only to find at daybreak that they are in the wrong spot.

First, be sure to put your decoys out in a natural manner — not too bunched up — because ducks bunch up only when they are afraid. Set your decoys in two loosely spaced groups leaving plenty of open water near your blind for the ducks to land.

A good way to set up decoys is across the wind with the wind coming in from left to right for right-handed shooters or vice versa for left-handed ones. This accomplishes two things: first, it provides you with shots that allow easy swinging from left to right, and second, crossing shots are the most dependable for ducks because vital areas are exposed and the bird provides a big profile.

Remember that ducks will generally come onto a marsh by heading into the wind. By setting your decoys on the lee side, you accomplish two things: the ducks will see the decoys from a long way, and they will find the lee inviting because pond ducks do not like sitting on rough water. Also, decoys generally do not ride realistically in rough water.

A dozen decoys — odd numbers such as 9 or 11 are preferred by some duck hunters — are plenty. Mallard decoys are the best because they will decoy all other species except perhaps blacks who are very wary and hard to fool. For black duck shooting 3 or 4 decoys are enough. Flocks of blacks will not generally decoy, but pairs and singles may.

Always build your blind carefully and out of local reeds or brush so that it is inconspicuous. Do not bring in strange reeds or grass. These will look out of place. Ducks spot "things that weren't there yesterday" very quickly. The best blind is a thick stand of natural vegetation.

Calling is very helpful if you are good. Otherwise forget it. One bad note is all it takes. Most beginning duck hunters call much too often and much too loudly. To become a good duck caller takes practice. If you are not willing to devote time to learning it, forget about it.

Dabbling ducks can also be jump shot. In my boyhood, I shot my share of ducks by walking from one country pond to another. When approaching a pond, slip in quietly, using any trees, brush, or fence rows for cover.

Don't hesitate to crawl if that's the only way to get close. Sometimes it's possible to hear ducks quacking as they are feeding on a farm pond or live-stock tank. I still bag a few ducks this way once in a while as a side light to a pheasant hunt.

Today, one of my favorite ways to jump shoot ducks is with a canoe on small, slow streams. I find that small streams are usually passed up by other hunters and I have them all to myself. Sometimes I can combine a duck hunt with a grouse or woodcock hunt. Good grouse and woodcock covers some-times border on streams. Other hunters find that squirrels can be taken as a side bag to a duck float.

Pass shooting and stubble shooting are also possible for dabblers, but more about this later.

One of the unique ways to hunt pond ducks is with a tolling dog. This

11. Without ducks, the hunting picture on this continent would be very bleak. Yet there may come a time when ducks are very rare. Why? Because we are draining our wetlands at a phenomenal rate. Ducks need marshes or they cannot survive.

is how it's done. The hunter hides on a shore of a lake or pond with sitting ducks on it and tosses a dummy or a rubber ball to a dog on shore, letting the dog retrieve it. As the game continues, the ducks become curious and swim up for a closer look. When they are close enough, the hunter shoots. It is imperative that the tolling dog perform in a joyful fun-like manner, and not pay any attention to the ducks. Also, there must be no other hunters nearby to frighten the ducks.

As far as I know, tolling is practiced only in Nova Scotia where a special breed of rusty, fox-like dog, the Nova Scotia tolling retriever, was developed for this sport. I mention this sport mainly because it is such a different method of hunting ducks, not because it is popular.

A retrieving dog is invaluable for pond ducks, more so than for any other waterfowl hunting. Many ducks are wasted every season because they fall into reeds and log-infested beaver ponds where finding a dead bird, let alone a wounded one, is hard for a hunter without a dog. Many of us feel that duck hunters who use retrieving dogs should be allowed an extra duck on their bag limits as an inducement for others to obtain retrieving dogs.

A shotgun for decoy shooting on small marshes and ponds should have a fairly open choke, modified being perhaps the best. The shots are generally not long — rarely over 40 yards — unless, of course, you are hunting on a crowded marsh where invariably some fool opens up long before the ducks are in range. For pond duck shooting, No. 6 shot is a good choice, but some hunters prefer larger shot sizes. If the birds are mostly teal or wood ducks. 7½'s are even better. The gauge can be anything from a 12 to a 20.

THE DIVING DUCKS

The bay ducks, as diving ducks are sometimes called, generally live on big waters and feed by diving down below the surface. They can always be identified by the relatively large-lobed hind toe. When taking off, the diving ducks head into the wind and patter over the water surface until they are air-borne. Their relatively small wings do not allow them to spring up from water in the same manner as the pond ducks. The diving ducks sometimes dive to great depths to feed, and are capable of swimming long distances under water.

THE CANVASBACK   *Aythya valisineria*

Identification — The drake canvasback is characterized by a dark chestnut-red head, a black chest, and a white body. The hen is brownish in color with a grey back. Both sexes have brown wings with grey patches. Another identifying feature of this duck is a wedge-shaped bill and a sloping forehead. The mature canvasback weighs about 2¾ pounds.

The canvasback breeds from the southern Mackenzie River Delta south to the Canada-U.S. border, and south to northern Utah in the west and central Nebraska in the mid-west. Its breeding range runs from western Minnesota to eastern Washington, with a small patch of breeding territory in Alaska and the Yukon.

THE REDHEAD
Aythya americana

Identification — The drake has a distinctive chestnut red head, a black chest, white breast, and dark grey body. The hen has a brownish body with a white breast. The wings of both sexes are grey-brown with grey wing patches. The redhead is also characterized by a pronounced forehead. A mature redhead runs about 2¼ pounds.

The breeding range of the redhead extends from northern Alberta and Saskatchewan to central Washington and Montana in the west and southern Nebraska in the mid-west. The bird breeds from eastern Minnesota to eastern British Columbia with small patches of breeding territory in Utah-Idaho and Oregon-California-Nevada.

THE BLUEBILLS
Aythya spp.

Identification — Only the greater scaup and the lesser scaup are generally regarded as "true" bluebills. However, as many sportsmen frequently consider the ring-necked duck as a bluebill, I have included it here.

The drake ring-necked duck *(Aythya collaris)* is characterized by a black head glossed with purple, a black chest, and a black back glossed with green. A ring or collar of chestnut, as both the common and specific names indicate, exists around the neck, but can only be seen at close range. The blue bill of this duck has a distinct white band near the tip, giving the duck the name of ring-bill on occasion. The hen is sooty brown in color with a white ring near the tip of the slate-grey bill. Both sexes have grey wing patches and weigh about 1½ pounds.

The greater scaup *(Aythya marila)* has a dark blue bill. The drake has a black head and chest. The back is pale grey and the sides are finely barred with black. The hen is brown, shading to light brown on the flanks and white on the breast. The hen has a prominent white patch at the base of the beak. Both sexes possess distinct white wing patches and generally run about 2 pounds.

The lesser scaup *(Aythya affinis)* is slightly smaller than the greater scaup; however, this is hard to see unless both species are in hand. The drake lesser scaup has a purplish sheen which the greater scaup lacks. The white wing patches on both sexes of the lesser scaup are smaller than those of the greater scaup. The lesser scaup weighs about 1¾ pounds, only ¼ pound less than the greater scaup.

The ringneck breeds from south of the Great Slave Lake to central Alberta and Saskatchewan in the west and the western Great Lakes in the east. It also nests in New Brunswick and Maine. The greater scaup nests from northern Saskatchewan right through the Mackenzie River Delta to the Bering Sea. The lesser scaup breeds from western Ontario to central British Columbia and from the Mackenzie River Delta to southern Nebraska.

THE GOLDENEYES   *Bucephala* spp.

Identification — Both species of goldeneyes — the common and the Barrow's — are sometimes called whistlers.

The drake common goldeneye *(Bucephala clangula)*, sometimes known as the American goldeneye, is a black and white bird with a black head glossed with green. It has a prominent white spot between the eye and the beak. The black wings have large white patches. The hen has an ash grey and white body with a brown head. The grey wings have small white patches.

The Barrow's goldeneye *(Bucephala islandica)* is quite similar. The black head of the drake has a purple sheen and a white crescent between the eye and the bill. This white crescent is a good identifying mark. The Barrow's goldeneye hen is difficult to distinguish from the common goldeneye hen. Both species weigh about 1¾ pounds.

The breeding range of the common goldeneye is a wide strip running from the Bering Sea on the coast of Alaska southeast through the Canadian prairies and the northern Great Lakes area to the Canadian Maritime Provinces. The Barrow's goldeneye breeds from the southern Yukon south to central California in the west and central Colorado. Minor breeding populations are also found along the coast of Labrador, the southern coast of Greenland, and in Iceland.

THE BUFFLEHEAD   *Bucephala albeola*

Identification — The bufflehead is the smallest of our diving ducks. The drake is unmistakably characterized by a large "buffle" head comprising a white patch extending from the eye to the back of the head. The body is white with the center of the back being black. The black wings have an extensive white patch on their inner half. The female bufflehead has a sooty brown body and head, with a prominent white cheek patch behind the eye. The bufflehead runs about the size of a teal, about 12 ounces.

The bufflehead breeds over a fairly wide range from western Alaska south to northern California, through the Canadian prairies to the northern Great Lakes area.

THE RUDDY DUCK   *Oxyura jamaicensis*

Identification — The drake ruddy duck is a rich chestnut red in color. His head has a black cap, white cheeks, and a bright blue bill. This small and attractive duck weighs only an ounce or two over a pound. The hen is mottled dark brown, with a brown cap and dullish white cheeks divided by a brown bar on her head, and a grey bill.

The ruddy duck breeds from central Alberta and Saskatchewan south to Utah in the west and Kansas in the mid-west, with a minor breeding population in northern California and Nevada.

THE HARLEQUIN DUCK   *Histrionicus histrionicus*
Identification — The drake harlequin duck is a striking slate blue bird with chestnut sides and an intricate pattern of white spots and stripes edged in black on the head, neck, and chest. The wings are dark slate with a tinge of blue. The female is sooty brown with white spots in front of the eyes and white cheeks. The harlequin duck runs about 1¼ pounds.

The harlequin has two breeding populations, an eastern one and a western one. The eastern population breeds along the shore of Labrador and northern Quebec, on eastern Baffin Island, and on the coasts of Greenland and Iceland. The western population breeds along the southern shore of Alaska south to central Oregon and west to Montana and Wyoming.

THE OLDSQUAW   *Clangula hyemalis*
Identification — The drake oldsquaw has two distinct color phases. In winter, the bird has a white head and neck with a dark cheek patch circling the eye. It also has two white stripes on its back near the wings. In summer, the white on the head, neck, and back turns dark brown, while the dark cheek patch around the eye becomes whitish. The drake always has long striking tail feathers similar to the pintail. The hen lacks these long tail feathers and is generally mottled brown with considerable white on her cheeks and chin. The oldsquaw generally weighs about 1½ pounds.

The oldsquaw is a Maritime duck, breeding mainly on the Arctic coast from the eastern tip of Labrador to the western tip of Alaska, including the Arctic islands. The bird winters on the coast of British Columbia, the Atlantic coast of New England, and in the Great Lakes area.

THE MERGANSERS   *Mergus* spp. and *Lophodytes cucullatus*
Identification — Three species of mergansers breed in North America — the common, the red-breasted, and the hooded. All the mergansers can be readily identified by their long, saw-like bills.

The common merganser *(Mergus merganser)*, sometimes referred to as the American merganser, is the biggest of the mergansers, weighing almost 2½ pounds. The drake has a dark back with light underside and a glossy, green-black head. The bird also has a white neck band. The feet and bill are red. The hen has a chestnut head, a grey back, and a white breast.

The red-breasted merganser drake *(Mergus serrator)* is similar in appearance to the common merganser, but has a striking crest on its head. Its breast is pinkish with black spots. The hen is also similar to the common

97

merganser hen, but like the drake, she does have a crest on her head. The red-breasted merganser weighs about 1¾ pounds.

The hooded merganser *(Lophodytes cucullatus)* is the handsomest of the three. The drake's most striking feature is a fan-shaped crest on a black head. The female is a greyish brown duck with a white breast, and also has a crest on her head, but much smaller than that of the male. The hooded merganser is the smallest of the three, averaging about 1¼ pounds.

The breeding range of the commmon merganser extends in a wide band across the Canadian prairies from coast to coast. The common merganser will inhabit salt and brackish water bogs in winter, but not to the same extent as the red-breasted merganser.

The red-breasted merganser breeds in all of the Canadian provinces from the eastern coast of Newfoundland through the Canadian prairies and the Northwest Territories to the western coast of Alaska. The hooded merganser has a similar range. It breeds from central British Columbia south to northern Oregon and southeast in a wide band to the Atlantic coast.

HUNTING THE DIVING DUCKS

I know of no other hunting sport that subjects the participants to more discomfort than hunting diving ducks. Diver shooting reaches its peak in the late fall when the marrow-chilling north winds sweep down over much of the country, and the hardy, fast-flying diving ducks move south. Divers always seem to move in with severe storms, almost as if they enjoyed riding the wind and sleet.

Somehow the cold, semi-darkness of dawn, whitecaps rolling over a swift wind, and ice-encrusted decoys — lots of them — are part of the game. At the prospect of a shotgun sport that is hard to surpass, many of us endure weather that would freeze the fires of hell. Hunting diving ducks is a specialized, open water sport. It requires boats, motors, and large sets of decoys. The same common sense applies in hunting divers as in hunting dabblers.

It is always wise to set your raft of decoys in an area where you have seen birds feeding or in a known feeding area. Since diving ducks fly in large flocks, you will need much larger rafts of decoys to bring them in for a look. Sets of 60 decoys are about minimum, and twice that many are better. Always set your decoys into the wind, leaving an empty space close to your blind because diving ducks always take off into the wind to give themselves an extra lift.

When a flock of divers is looking over your decoys, watch their feet. If they are going to set down, they will start trailing their feet while still some distance away. However, if their feet are tucked away you can be sure that they will only buzz your decoys. In this case give the birds plenty of lead when you shoot. They will pick up speed as they fly over your decoys.

I believe in soundly built blinds that conceal the hunters well. The blinds should be built or anchored out in the water before the divers come south. This tactic may not be as necessary for bluebills and redheads because they generally decoy much more readily — even stupidly — as for canvasbacks. Canvasbacks can be cagey and difficult to lure in. You need all the breaks you can get for "cans". However, with today's low limits on canvasbacks, any extra trouble is probably not worth it.

Bluebills are the mainstay of diving duck shooting today, with golden-eyes and buffleheads providing an extra bit of variety. Oldsquaws are sometimes included in a bag, but they are principally fish eaters and hunters who know their ducks seldom bother with them.

THE SEA DUCKS

THE SCOTERS
Oidemia nigra and *Melanitta* spp.

Identification — The scoters are comprised of three species — the white-winged scoter, the surf scoter, and the black scoter.

The white-winged scoter drake *(Melanitta deglandi)* is black with prominent white wing patches and white crescent-shaped markings around the eyes. The hen is a dark sooty brown with white wing patches. The white-wing is the biggest of the scoters, weighing about 2¾ pounds.

The surf scoter *(Melanitta perspicillata)* is also black with prominent white patches on the forehead. The hen is sooty brown with white spots at the base of the bill and sides of the head.

The black scoter *(Oidemia nigra)*, sometimes known as the American or common scoter, is the only duck in America with true black plumage. The drake is solid black with an orange swelling at the base of the bill. The hen is sooty brown with a black crown and a light grey face and throat. The black scoter, as well as the surf scoter, runs about 2 pounds.

The white-winged scoter has the largest breeding range, extending from the Mackenzie River Delta to northern Manitoba and North Dakota and from Lake Winnipeg west to western Alberta. The surf scoter breeds in the western Northwest Territories, the northern Yukon, and parts of Alaska. The black scoter breeds on the salt water coasts of the Bering and Beaufort Sea.

THE EIDERS
Somateria spp. and others

Identification — There are four species of eiders common to North America — the common eider, the king eider, the spectacled eider, and the Steller's eider.

The drake common eider *(Somateria mollissima)*, sometimes called the American eider, is a striking black and white duck. The black head has a greenish gloss with a slight dip to the bill. The hen is dark brown with black bars.

99

The king eider *(Somateria spectabilis)* is also a striking duck. The drake is white on the foreparts and black on the rear parts. The top of the head and neck are bluish grey. The hen is brown and very much resembles the common eider hen, but is somewhat brighter in color.

The drake spectacled eider *(Lampronetta fischeri)* has a faded green head with large white "spectacles" around the eyes. This black-breasted bird is extremely attractive. The female is similar in appearance to the common eider, but also has the spectacles, although they are somewhat faded. The bill of both sexes is feathered over the nostril.

The drake Steller's eider *(Polysticta stelleri)*, in its breeding plumage, is a handsome bird with unusual markings. He has a white head with a black throat. Black coloring separates the neck from the body. This black coloring overflows to the back as a black stripe. The sides, including the wings, have a fair amount of white. The female is predominantly brown. Her wing is similar to that of the mallard. Both sexes have small crests on the back of the head. The Steller's eider is the smallest of the eiders, weighing about 2 pounds. The other eiders range from 3½ to 4 pounds.

The common eider's breeding range extends from northern Connecticut through the Canadian maritime provinces to the coast of Labrador, as well as along the eastern and western coasts of Hudson Bay and through many of the Arctic islands. The breeding area of the king eider stretches from the western coast of Alaska right across the top of Canada through all the Arctic islands to Greenland.

The spectacled eider breeds along the northern coast of Alaska. This eider was never abundant on the North American continent; however, it is a common sea duck along the coast of Siberia. The Steller's eider has much the same breeding range as the spectacled eider, and again, is also more common in Siberia than in North America.

HUNTING THE SEA DUCKS

Hunting "coots" as scoters are called along the Atlantic coast has a small but dedicated following. [Along with the scoters the larger eiders are sometimes taken.] Scoters tend to prefer bay water while eiders are offshore ducks. This is one reason scoters are subjected to more hunting. [The more important reason is that the eiders are basically northern birds, out of the reach of most hunters.] The king and common eiders winter off the coast of eastern Canada and New England, but no farther south. Scoters, on the other hand, winter from eastern Canada right down to the Carolinas and hence offer more hunting opportunities.

The sea ducks, particularly the scoters, are not very wary. A canvasback hunter would consider them downright stupid. They will decoy to just about anything if they have not been too heavily gunned. Wooden blocks — not even proper decoys — are frequently used. In the old days, large cork floats from fishing nets frequently served as coot decoys. Some hunters use silhouette decoys, "shadows" as they are locally called, each nailed onto an individual board and strung on a series. A hunter after sea ducks can sit up in his boat and not conceal himself. All he has to do is sit still. The birds may sometimes circle and then drop in behind the gunner. Experience soon teaches the coot hunter how to handle such situations.

Scoters, however, are fast-flying birds usually flying in line just barely skimming the water. They rise into the air only when an obstacle — a boat or a point of land — is in their line of flight.

A good place to hunt coots is in a bay that has a headland thrusting out into the sea. If there is a group of hunters with boats, the boats should be anchored in a line about 100 yards apart, each with its own set of decoys. Scoters, as they pass, will decoy to one set, and as they are fired on, will fly to the next set instead of passing and flying away.

Almost any kind of stable boat can be used for coot hunting. The old wooden dories and skiffs are still used by some of the old-timers. The boats should be painted dull colors. When a pair of gunners are hunting from one boat, they should sit back to back. In this way they will have the whole field covered. In some years it is possible to gun coots from low, offshore points. A boat is still needed, however, to retrieve the birds.

Sea ducks are hard birds to kill. A full-choked hard hitting 12 gauge with a stiff load of No. 4 shot is best. Some hunters prefer smaller shot as the first load or in the more open bore of a double. When gunning sea ducks, it is wise to bring plenty of shells.

Sea ducks likewise are not generally regarded as our finest table birds. Most hunters eat only the breasts. There is actually very little meat on the rest of the bird. It is frequently said that you have to be born on the coast to appreciate sea ducks on the dinner plate. When the breasts are slowly simmered in mushroom gravy or in a wine sauce, they can be quite tasty.

THE GEESE

THE CANADA GOOSE   *Branta canadensis*

Identification — The Canada goose is so widely known that it hardly needs to be described. It is a large brownish grey bird with a long neck. The head and neck are skinny, black in color, and interrupted by an oval patch of white on the upper sides of the head and cheek and under the throat. The breast is pale ash-grey. The sexes cannot be differentiated by their coloring.

The Canada goose has several sub-species or races, all of which look essentially alike except for minor variations in color. The major difference in these sub-species is in size. The largest race of Canada goose is the giant Canada, weighing up to 14 pounds. The smallest, the cackling Canada, is not much larger than a mallard.

12. The Canada goose is the "big game" of waterfowl hunting. It is widely distributed and most abundant of all the geese, but it is alert, shy, and never easy to hunt.

The Canada goose, sometimes colloquially known as the "honker", flies in the familiar "V" formation on long flights, but short local flights are not usually flown in formation.

The breeding range of Canada geese extends from Newfoundland through Labrador and around the coast of Hudson Bay into southern Ontario, where breeding flocks have been established. The birds also breed from north of the Great Slave Lake south to southern Utah and Colorado and from western Wisconsin to Vancouver Island.

THE SNOW GOOSE
Chen hyperborea

Identification — The snow goose is a fairly large white bird with black wing tips. The head, neck, and undersides can be a little rust colored, while the legs and feet are pink. Immature snow geese have a greyish colored head and neck, with grey wings. Both sexes look alike.

The snow goose also has a blue phase which is sometimes called the blue goose. At one time, ornithologists considered the blue goose a separate species *(Chen caerulescens)*, and in most bird guides, the blue goose is still listed as such, but the majority of waterfowl biologists consider it a color phase of the snow. The blue phase has a bluish colored body with bluish grey wings. The neck and head are white. The bill has a black "grinning patch" between the mandibles. There are two races of snow geese — the lesser snow goose weighing less than 5 pounds and the greater snow goose weighing a pound or so more. Aside from size, these birds are essentially the same in appearance and have the same identifying marks.

The lesser snow goose breeds along the Arctic coast of Alaska and the Northwest Territories to Hudson Bay and on Baffin Island. The greater snow goose breeds from northern Baffin Island to western Greenland.

THE WHITE-FRONTED GOOSE *Anser albifrons*

Identification — The white-fronted goose, sometimes known as the specklebelly, is not a widely known goose. Its head, neck, back, and rump are greyish brown. The forehead is white. The tail is dark brown edged in white. The breast and belly are greyish and heavily blotched with dark brown, hence the name specklebelly. The legs and feet of the white-front are orange. Both sexes are similar in appearance, with an average weight of a little less than 5 pounds.

The whitefront breeds in northern Alaska and along the Arctic coast of the Yukon and the Northwest Territories to Victoria Island, as well as on Greenland along the Davis Strait.

THE ROSS'S GOOSE *Chen rossii*

Identification — The Ross's goose is similar in appearance to the snow goose, only a bit smaller. It runs on the average about 2¾ pounds. Both sexes look alike, being white birds with black wing tips. The bill is pinkish, and in adult birds has wart-like protuberances between the nostril and the base. The bill of the Ross's goose is also shorter than that of the snow goose and lacks the grinning patch. Every hunter should know the Ross's goose well because it is fully protected.

Until 1938, the breeding ground of the Ross's goose was unknown. It was discovered by Angus Gavin on the Perry River of the Northwest Territories. The bird winters in the Sacramento and San Joachim Valleys of California.

THE EMPEROR GOOSE *Philacte canagica*

Identification — The emperor goose is regarded by many to be our most beautiful goose. The predominant body color is bluish grey. The head and the back of the neck are white, but the throat is deep brown. The feathers on the back, flanks, and breast have black, crescent-shaped markings and are tipped with white. The feet are orange-yellow, while the bill may vary from pale purple to flesh colored. Both sexes look alike.

The emperor goose breeds along the coastline of Alaska's Bering Sea and winters in the Alaska Peninsula.

13. The emperor goose is our most beautiful goose. It breeds along the northern coast of Alaska and winters along the coast of southern Alaska. Because it inhabits such remote areas, it is rarely hunted.

THE BRANT

Branta bernicla

Identification — The brant is a small dark sea goose with a white head, neck, and chest. The back and upper sides of the wings are brown, while the wing tips are blackish. The rump and tail are black. The belly and sides are brownish grey. There is a narrow white crescent on either side of the neck just below the head. The sexes are similar in appearance, and the birds run about 2½ to 3 pounds.

Brant nest from the eastern shore of Hudson Bay and Baffin Island west to the Bering Strait. The wintering habitats are salt water bays, from Chesapeake Bay to the Carolinas on the Atlantic coast and from southern British Columbia to Baja California. Concentrations of wintering birds tend to be greater at the more southerly latitudes. The brant will also stop over in inland lakes and rivers and even fields during migration.

Incidentally, in some bird guides the Pacific coast brant is called the black brant *(Branta nigricans)* because it is somewhat darker, particularly the immature birds. Waterfowl biologists consider the west and east coast brant to be separate races, but not separate species.

HUNTING THE GEESE

The honking of wild geese is a siren song to a goose hunter. The plaintive honk is a symbol of wilderness. It represents life in the wild, free places that only a hunter can appreciate, but rarely fully understand. To some hunters, geese are an irresistible magnet. They have the same sort of attraction that wild turkeys have to other hunters. Wild geese are the big game of waterfowl hunting.

Because wild geese nest in the far north, on land still untouched by man, they have fared well in this century. All they need is some protection in the form of bag limits and seasons and they respond. Our goose flocks have been increasing in numbers. We probably have more geese today than when your father or grandfather were hunting them. If we can keep the remote north clean and undisturbed, we will always have geese.

Goose hunting can be full of contrasts. On the Hudson and James Bay coasts, snow geese are so unsophisticated that they will decoy to lumps of mud and sheets of newspaper folded over marsh grass. Without the expert calling of the Cree Indian guides, success would, of course, not be as easy. However, the fact remains that this is the easiest goose hunting to be had. This is why perhaps it loses its charm and lure so quickly. Everything that comes easily soon ceases to be exciting. The most captivating part of a Hudson or James Bay goose hunt is the country — the wild, desolate landscape where the wild goose lives and rears its young. Every waterfowler should go there once.

Hunting honkers on the wheat stubbles of Manitoba or the corn fields of Maryland is another matter. Everything has to be perfect or it will not work. The right field has to be chosen. The pit has to be dug carefully and in the right place. No fresh earth can be left around to warn the birds. The decoys must be set just right. Finally, when the birds are flying, the calling has to be perfect, without a single false note. The hunters and dogs must be perfectly still until the right moment when the geese are in shotgun range.

Goose hunting is rarely done over water, except, of course, for brant. Most of the goose hunting is done over feeding areas, either grassy meadows or tide flats, but more often grain fields. The technique is a simple one. Locate the area where the birds are feeding and be there before they arrive the following day. The only way to locate feeding birds is to be out looking with binoculars. When such a field is located, you must get the farmer's permission to dig a pit. Be sure to fill in the pit completely after your hunt, or neither you or anyone else will ever be allowed to hunt there again.

The decoys must be spread out to represent a feeding flock of geese. Some of the decoys must have resting heads, other must have feeder heads, and a few must have alert upright heads. Some geese are always looking up whenever a flock feeds. But too many decoys with their heads up means unrest and caution to oncoming birds.

When you spot birds on the horizon, start calling and take cover immediately in the pit. If you are not an expert caller, stop calling as soon as the birds are close or as soon as they head for your decoys. A single false note will spoil everything.

Don't shoot until the birds are within range. This can be tricky because the birds are big. They frequently appear closer than they are. They also fly faster than most hunters realize. Be sure to lead them enough.

Pass shooting for geese is not frequently done, largely because the birds fly high until they come down into the fields. But occasionally it is possible to pass shoot in foul or foggy weather when the birds stay low. Geese generally spend the nights on big lakes. If you want to pass shoot geese, this is where you should look.

Hunting brant is very specialized. It is generally done over water in areas where these sea geese are known to feed on eelgrass. Scouting the seashore for feeding brant or stands of eelgrass is the best way to start. Brant decoys are nearly always used. Brant can also be pass shot from rocky points jutting out into the sea. Brant do not like to fly far from shore. This is a real bonus for the pass shooter.

The best guns for geese are full-choked 12 gauges, but a 3-inch 20 magnum is also suitable. I am against 10 gauge magnums because few of us today are good long range shots. The best shot size is a point of debate. No. 4 shot is ample for much goose shooting, but big honkers at times require No. 2's. BB's are only rarely needed.

A dog is not needed for hunting geese because wounded birds never hide.

However, I always use my dog because hunting with a dog is more enjoyable. Once a dog learns how to pick up and carry a big Canada, mallards are a snap.

SPECIAL FORMS OF
WATERFOWL GUNNING
Pass Shooting

Pass shooting is the hardest type of waterfowl gunning. The birds are generally flying much faster than those settling in to decoys and the ranges are considerably longer. It is a somewhat simple form of waterfowl hunting, since decoys are not used. The hunter locates a "pass", a local flyway which the ducks use daily on their way to and from feeding and roosting areas. The hunter then finds some suitable cover, hides, and waits for the birds to start moving.

A good pass can be a creek or a narrow neck of water between two marshes. The shortest route between marshes or lakes and grain fields of farm country can also be a good pass. Pass shooting can also be practiced in rough, windy weather. On the sea coast, reefs and breakers or points of land jutting into the water can be good passes. The birds in this case will be "trading" more than usual, trying to find a sheltered place.

The main problem with inland pass shooting, aside from finding a good pass, is other hunters. As soon as the gunning pressure increases a bit, the ducks change their flyway or fly high. They may even learn to fly high before and after the legal shooting time. This is why pass shooting is not practiced as much today as in the past.

All pass shooting requires a full-choked gun and heavy loads. This is where the magnums come into their own. Pass shooting is an extremely difficult form of gunning. Our limits are just too small for most of us to develop the skill and experience required to hit waterfowl consistently at long ranges. Today we have guns capable of killing ducks at 60 or even 70 yards, but most of us just aren't 60 yard shooters.

Stubble Shooting

Geese and dabbling ducks can both be hunted on stubble fields. Ducks, particularly mallards, and geese, particularly Canadas, love grain. They will feed on grain in preference to anything else. Big corn fields are the reason why Maryland has such fine goose shooting today. Geese have changed their migration habits because of the corn. They just don't migrate as far south. On the Canadian prairies, ducks do considerable damage to standing wheat in some areas, so much so that the Canadian government is paying farmers an indemnity for the damage caused.

The key to good stubble shooting is to locate the areas where the birds are feeding. Then the hunter must be there well ahead of the flight to set up his decoys and dig his pit. Most of us prefer to dig our pits the night before. For duck stubble shooting, it is sometimes possible to use a low blind built of straw and weeds in a fence row or on the edge of a shelter belt. Geese, however, seldom land near fences or shelter belts. They are too wise.

For a morning shoot, the hunter must be in his blind well before the first hint of light. A duck stubble shoot on the Canadian prairies is something that lightens the heart of any waterfowler. With the first hint of light, seemingly endless strings of mallards move out from the sloughs and marshes. Occasionally small flocks of other duck species can be seen — pintails, or perhaps baldpates and gadwalls.

Most of the ducks are flying into other fields, other designations. Suddenly a string of mallards peels off and heads for your decoys. They pass high, but then wheel and circle. One more circle and you will have them. Their undersides are pale now. Four shots ring out, and three ducks plummet to the stubble.

The dog behind you trembles with excitement. He wants to contribute to the hunt. He wants to inhale the enticing scent of a warm mallard and feel it in his soft jaws. But he sits. The command "fetch" has not been given. The flight will last another 30 minutes. The time for retrieving will come afterwards.

It has to be a crown day for a stubble shooter to get his limit, but the success of the hunt is not measured by limits. You and your partner have shot two mallards each. The flight is over. Major's work will now begin. A dog is almost a must on a stubble shoot, because a wounded mallard will sulk off and hide with the skill of a pheasant. Major has no trouble finding the birds. You fill your pit, because the ducks will not be back in this field for at least a few days. The hunt is over.

For evening stubble shooting, the hunters must be in their blinds or pits while the sun is still high. The ducks will not start moving until just about dusk, but there is a chance that the odd straggler, a single or a pair, may move early. You must pick up your downed ducks early, while there is still enough light to see them, in the stubble.

Hunting Canadas over stubble can be exasperating. The technique is the same as for ducks, but you have to be sharper and a bit more clever. Fresh earth near the pit can make the geese shy away, particularly if they've been shot at. When geese are heavily gunned, they become extremely wary. They refuse to decoy. They actually avoid any "flocks" on the ground. They seldom feed in one field on two consecutive days.

One of the best ways to find stubble fields that geese are using is to follow flocks of geese in the late afternoon or early morning with a car. This, of course, works only if there are enough country roads. Binoculars are also very helpful. When you find a field that geese are using, the next step is to get the farmer's permission to hunt there and to dig a pit. This can be difficult. If permission is given, you are in business.

One word of advice. Always fill in your pits after the hunt. A small minority of hunters don't, and they are ruining stubble shooting for the rest of us. Once a farmer is forced to fill in the pits himself, he will probably never allow another hunter to shoot the stubble.

Sculling

Sculling is another duck hunting technique. It can be considered as a specialized form of duck shooting. The scull boat is a boat with an extremely low profile. The gunner lies down in the boat and propels it forward with a scull oar in the stern.

When a flock of ducks is spotted on the water, the sculler propels the boat slowly forward towards the ducks, hoping to get within shotgun range. Some hunters mount a seagull on the bow of the scull boat to make the boat look like a large piece of flotsam. A few scullers have completely white scull boats for ice festooned waters.

Any type of duck can be hunted in this way. Sculling, however, can only be practiced on calm water. Waves would break over the gunwales of the scull boat, soaking the hunter and filling the boat with water. Large rivers, sheltered lakes and bays, and big marshes are the best places to scull for ducks.

Sculling is not practiced a great deal. A few devotees, however, still scull for ducks in New England and the northern seaboard states.

Chapter IX

Shore and Marsh Birds

Shore and marsh bird hunting as it was practiced before the turn of the century is a thing of the past. Comparatively few hunters venture out after rails today, and indeed, most shore birds are protected. The snipe and woodcock are two exceptions. I have included the woodcock in the chapter on upland game birds because the timberdoodle is hunted in the uplands. However, scientifically speaking, the woodcock is a shore bird. The common snipe may still be hunted, but it is not a popular game bird.

At one time birds such as the black-bellied plover, the golden plover, the upland plover, and the greater yellow legs were much sought after game birds by market hunters. All of these species are still quite abundant, but, of course, not as in the past. The golden plover is still hunted to a minor extent in Mexico. One shore bird species, the Eskimo curlew, was nearly brought to extinction by market hunters.

THE COMMON SNIPE *Capella gallinago*

Identification — The common snipe, or Wilson's snipe as it is more commonly called, resembles a thin, small woodcock. Its long straight bill and thin legs are similar to those of the woodcock. The upper parts of the common snipe are mixed brown, buff, ochre, and blackish with buff stripes down the back. The breast is buffy brown with dusky markings, and the belly is white. The flanks and sides are barred with blackish brown.

Hunting Hints — The open wetlands, moist meadows, mud flats, edges of marshes and bogs are the places to hunt these birds. Avoid thick cover and reeds with standing water. During the fall migration, snipe will inhabit wet fields or edges of ponds particularly where livestock have trampled down the vegetation. The best way to hunt the bird is to walk slowly through likely looking snipe habitat. A flushing dog is useful, and some pointing dogs also learn to point snipe. A retrieving dog is of immense value because a snipe downed in a clump of thick vegetation can be hard to find.

14. *The snipe, with its erratic, weaving flight, is difficult to hit. These birds hanging on the loops of my German hunting pouch were bagged along Quebec's Isle aux Grues.*

The common snipe is a fast bird on the wing. It flies with an erratic zig-zag flight which makes for sporty shooting. A good snipe gun should be light and open bored. However, a double with one barrel of a tighter choke than the other is even better because some of the shots can be long. The best shot is No. 9, but 8's or 7½'s can be used.

Snipe are considered by some gourmets to be our finest tasting game bird. I, personally, prefer bobwhite quail.

Snipe can be hunted in almost every state and province. Indeed its distribution is almost world-wide, and snipe is a highly sought after game bird by European hunters. In North America, the mud flats of James Bay in Ontario, the islands and tidal flats of the Gulf of St. Lawrence around Quebec City, and the edges of coastal marshes in Louisiana are well known for their concentrations of snipe.

THE RAILS   *Rallus* spp. and others

Identification — The rails are a very interesting group of marsh birds. The term "skinny as a rail" comes from the fact that these birds are thin and capable of slipping through reeds. Four species of rails — the king rail, the clapper rail, the Virginia rail, and the sora rail — are normally hunted in North America. The latter species is the most abundant.

The sora rail *(Porzana carolina)* is a small chunky bird about three quarters the size of a woodcock. It has a short yellowish bill. Its upper parts are olive brown streaked with black. The breast is grey and the throat is black. The sora lives principally in fresh water marshes, but can be found in brackish water marshes as well.

The Virginia rail *(Rallus limicola)* is a shade bigger than the sora. It is a cinnamon-breasted bird with a long slender reddish bill and greyish cheeks. The Virginia rail inhabits both fresh and brackish water marshes.

The king rail *(Rallus elegans)* is similar in appearance to the Virginia rail, but does not have the grey cheeks of the Virginia and is twice the size. The king rail is found almost exclusively in fresh water marshes.

The clapper rail *(Rallus longirostris)* is a fairly large bird with a slightly downturned bill. It resembles a king rail but is a shade smaller. It is found principally in salt marshes.

Hunting Hints — The traditional method of rail hunting, with a push boat, has a small but faithful following. It was a sport for gentlemen gunners. George B. Grinnel, a noted conservationist who helped to found the first Audubon Society, was an enthusiastic rail hunter. The sport was developed in the early 1800's by shooters who enjoyed this leisurely and easy (physically and in terms of marksmanship) form of wing shooting. The tiny, wild rice fattened sora rail was even then a highly esteemed morsel. Anyone who has shot this small bird knows that a morsel is all it is. The sora is barely a mouthful.

113

Today the sora and Virginia rails are still hunted with a long, narrow push boat with a gunner seated on the stool in front and a pusher standing in the back. However, only a few pushers ply their trade on the Atlantic coast marshes. There are more dependable and lucrative ways to earn a living today.

I have hunted rails by taking turns paddling a canoe through marshes. This is a sort of modern version of the old push boat technique. I have also hunted rails by wading in marshes with chest waders. This is a hard way to bag rails, but it can be done. In the warm weather of early fall (rail seasons are frequently the first hunting seasons to open) a few hardy hunters along Long Island-New Jersey and in the south shun chest waders and wade in with old clothes and running shoes. There is no doubt that walking in such clothing is a bit easier. King rails are normally hunted by wading in the rice fields of Louisiana.

Rails have to be "cornered" in pockets of reeds against open water before they take to their wings. Not being fast or strong fliers, they are easy to hit. A light, open-choked shotgun with No. 9 shot is best for sora and Virginia rails. Somewhat larger shot sizes, perhaps 7½'s, are better for king and clapper rails. The rails, particularly the sora and Virginia, are fine game for the .410 fans. A retrieving dog is extremely useful because finding a downed rail in thick cover can be quite difficult.

The Atlantic seaboard states have been the traditional rail hunting areas. Most of the marshes in the Atlantic and Cumberland counties of New Jersey have fine rail gunning. The Patuxent marshes and the marshes of the Patapsco River in Maryland are excellent as well. The Connecticut River marshes also have good rail gunning. Clapper rails are found in the coastal marshes of North and South Carolina, Georgia, and Florida.

THE COOTS AND GALLINULES   *Rallidae*

Identification — Both the coots and gallinules are frequently referred to as mud hens or marsh hens by less discerning sportsmen. They are both dark grey marsh birds, about the size of small ducks, but with chicken-like bills. When swimming, their heads bob with each stroke.

There are two species of gallinules in North America. The common gallinule *(Gallinula chloropus)* has a reddish bill and a white line on its grey flank. Its breeding range extends from New England and the Great Lakes south through the mid-west to Florida and Texas. There is also an enclave of common gallinules along the California coast. The wintering range is the gulf coast from Texas to Florida and along the Gulf of California in Mexico.

The purple gallinule *(Porphyrula martinica)* is a southern bird. It has a dark green back with purple head, breast, and belly. It has a white plate on top of the forehead. In size and shape it is very similar to the common gallinule. The feet of the gallinules are chicken-like.

The purple gallinule nests from the Carolinas south through Florida and the coastal marshes of Louisiana and Texas. Its breeding range also extends up the lower Mississippi River valley. It winters from Florida and coastal Louisiana to Jamaica and tropical South America.

The American coot *(Fulica americana)* is a grey bird slightly larger than the gallinules. It has a white bill. In flight, the coot shows a flash of white on the hind edge of its wings. The foot of the coot has paddle-like lobes on its toes.

The coot's breeding range extends from New England to the Rocky Mountains and from the Great Slave Lake through the Great Plains to northern Mexico. In the east it winters on Chesapeake Bay south along the entire coast into Mexico. In the west it winters along the coast from British Columbia to Mexico. It also winters in the lower Mississippi valley.

Hunting Hints — The coots and gallinules are seldom intentionally hunted, but are sometimes bagged by duck hunters. Most waterfowlers, however, do not bother with them. They can be hunted by wading in the same manner as rails. However, paddling a canoe or a boat through a marsh is a better technique because coot and gallinule marshes may be on deeper water.

The coots and gallinules take to the wing fairly readily, but neither are fast fliers. Any open-choked shotgun with No. 6 or 7½ shot is a good bet. Neither of these birds have the fine flavor of the rails, but if skinned out rather than plucked, they can be quite tasty.

The coots and gallinules can be hunted just about anywhere in their range but the coastal marshes of Louisiana and Florida no doubt have the best coot and gallinule gunning. Coots are also abundant on the small marshes of the Canadian prairies.

THE SANDHILL CRANE   *Grus canadensis*

Identification — The sandhill crane is a large heronlike bird. It is predominantly slate colored with black wing tips. It flies with an outstretched neck and the upstroke of its wingbeat is rapid.

Hunting Hints — The sandhill crane was returned to the shooting list only a decade ago. Prior to this time it was protected for almost 50 years. One of the reasons why a limited open season is allowed in some states and Canadian provinces is because the birds have grown to such numbers that they are causing damage to grain fields.

When the sandhill seasons were opened again, most hunters did not have any idea how to hunt the bird. Several methods were attempted. Stalking birds that were feeding on stubble proved to be as difficult as stalking Canadas. One bird was always watching, and sandhills have very sharp eyesight.

Shooting over decoys was tried. To help with this, if my memory is correct, the New Mexico Department of Game and Fish published plans for making silhouette decoys. Perhaps these decoy plans are still in print. The decoy shooting did work. The sandhill is as wary as the Canada goose, and perhaps even more so. But if decoys are set up in a field where birds are feeding, and the hunters dig pits, they do stand a chance of getting some shooting. A goose gun, a full-choked 12 with a stiff load of No. 2 shot, is ideal for sandhills.

Pass shooting has also been tried with the hunters intercepting birds as they fly from roosting to feeding areas and vice versa. If the gunning pressure is not too intense, this can be a fairly successful method of hunting these long-legged birds. But after much gunning, the sandhills learn to fly high — very high.

At best, the sandhill is a minor game bird. Despite the fact that it is challenging to hunt, I doubt if it will ever be popular as a game bird. The four or five decades of closed season have erased much of the tradition of hunting this wary bird. I must admit that the only time I have shot the bird has been incidentally during hunts for other game. Only some of the western and mid-western states and western provinces have a season on the sandhill. Elsewhere it is fully protected.

Chapter X

Big Game

Big game hunting is a challenging and demanding pastime. By and large it requires greater expenditures in time and money than any other type of hunting. This does not, however, mean that a big game hunt is only for the affluent. A week-long deer hunt from Maine to Texas or a spring hunt for black bear in Canada is well within the financial reach of most hunters. But a trip into the Yukon mountains after Dall sheep and grizzly with a string of pack ponies is an expensive undertaking — $150 a day or more.

However, for a hunter who likes maximum challenge and has a great deal of perseverance and at times physical stamina, big game hunting is a magnet. It is not the kill that is the sole element. The kill, in fact, is frequently the anti-climax. The lure is in the game country of mountains and forests which stirs the blood, kindles the imagination, and haunts the soul of a hunter as he relives the life of his predatory ancestors.

THE DEER *Cervidae*

It may come as a surprise to many hunters that moose, elk, caribou, and the deer all belong to the deer family known as *Cervidae*. One common characteristic of this family is the possession of antlers by the males, except in caribou where both sexes are antlered.

A new pair of antlers is grown by deer family members every year. The old ones are shed during winter and the growth of the new ones begins in spring. Antler size depends on two things — the age of the animal and its diet. Generally antlers reach their biggest formation from 4 to 7 years, when the animal is in its prime. To grow big antlers, the animal must feed on plants growing in soil rich in calcium. Contrary to popular belief, the age of deer, moose, elk, or caribou cannot be told by the points or "tines" of the antlers. These animals must be aged by the wear on their teeth, as horses. Antlers have been regarded as a symbol of hunting prowess and a highly thought of trophy from time immemorial.

THE WHITE-TAILED DEER   *Odocoileus virginianus*

The white-tailed deer gets its name from the large white tail or "flag" which it carries upright when running. Its range is a wide one, extending from Nova Scotia to Washington and from Saskatchewan to Mexico. There are a number of geographic races of the whitetail such as the diminutive Key deer of the Florida Keys or the small and delicate Coues whitetail, sometimes called the fantail of southern New Mexico and Arizona and northern Mexico.

The average buck weighs about 175 pounds with the does being about 30 pounds lighter.

Hunting Hints — The whitetail is by far the wariest and most elusive of all our big game animals. Still hunting — walking very slowly on ridges

15. *Deer hunting with hounds is a pastime of ancient and honorable lineage. Today it is practiced only in the southern states and in Ontario, where this photo was taken. Here a hunter is being picked up after an unsuccessful deer chase.*

or game trails and stopping every few steps — is a good technique. Walk little and slowly. Look and listen a lot. Be sure to keep the wind in your favor because deer have good senses of smell. Taking a stand on a game trail is another good bet. Get on the stand early in the morning, well before daylight, and again in the afternoon because deer travel at dawn and dusk. Deer can also be driven past stands by groups of hunters. Deer drives are a popular hunting technique in some areas. In the south — below the Mason-Dixon line — and in Ontario, hounds can be used to chase deer past hunters on stands. Although many northern hunters may consider the deer chase unsporting, it is not. In thick swamps and forests it is the only effective way to hunt whitetails. A pack of hounds on the trail of a whitetail as it tries to sulk and give them the slip is a sound no hunter can forget.

Watch for game signs at all times — tracks, droppings, and battered saplings where bucks have rubbed the velvet off their antlers — when hunting. Plenty of signs indicate that you are in good deer country.

A good deer rifle for the eastern forests should be light and handy for quick shooting. The caliber is unimportant, but the larger calibers — .30 and up — are better for shooting through the brush. A hunter who bags a whitetail buck can feel proud indeed. It takes a good hunter to outwit and bag one.

Good whitetail hunting can occur just about anywhere in the animal's range. Florida, Louisiana, and Georgia have very fine deer hunting. Maine, Vermont, and New Brunswick are top places in the northeast. The mid-west has become fine whitetail country in recent years. Saskatchewan has outstanding deer hunting with plenty of big racks. But no doubt Texas is the best deer state of all. If you want to bag the Coues deer, Arizona is a good bet with northern Mexico perhaps being even better. The Coues whitetail, incidentally, has its own classification in the Boone and Crockett Club records because of its small size. The diminutive Keys deer is fully protected.

THE MULE DEER   *Odocoileus hemionus*

The mule deer gets its name from its large pair of ears which twist forward when the deer is alert. The muley runs with a peculiar jumping gait which is completely different from the wave-like leaping gait of the whitetail. The muley is a western deer. Its range extends from the Dakotas and Nebraska to Washington and California and from northern Alberta to northern Mexico including Baja California. The average muley buck weighs about 220 pounds, but 350-pound deer have been shot. The does run about 60 pounds lighter than the bucks.

Hunting Hints — Stalking is the best technique for hunting mule deer. The hunter must get up into high country before dawn and be out glassing the countryside with a pair of good binoculars at daybreak. At this time the muley bucks will be going back into the hillside thickets or treed ravines to spend the day. When the hunter has located the bedding place of a deer, he must go in, keeping the wind in his favor, and jump the deer. In forest country, a still hunt by walking slowly and stopping to look and listen frequently is a good technique. But most mule deer are found in semi-open country or at least that's where most hunters prefer to hunt.

During midday when the deer are generally bedded down, the hunter should poke his head into every conceivable clump of cover — bushy ravines, patches of tall shrubs on hillsides, small stands of evergreens. Nothing should be overlooked. This type of hunt works better with a partner. One man goes in while the other stays on the outside in case a buck bursts out.

A good mule deer rifle should be relatively flat shooting and accurate. The shots can be long ones when compared to those on white-tailed deer. Any caliber from .243 to .30 is a good bet.

Fine mule deer hunting can be found in just about all of the western states. Montana, Wyoming, and Idaho are good mule deer states. Fine mule deer hunting also exists in the interior of British Columbia. Colorado, Arizona, New Mexico, and Nevada all have fine deer hunting in some areas, but Utah is probably the top mule deer state.

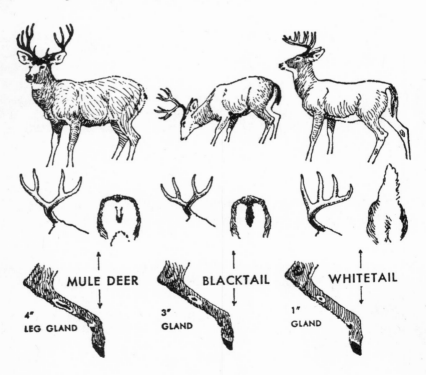

MULE DEER   BLACKTAIL   WHITETAIL

4"   3"   1"
LEG GLAND   GLAND   GLAND

THE BLACK-TAILED DEER   *Odocoileus hemionus*

The blacktail, formerly thought to be a completely different species, is really a subspecies of the mule deer. It should perhaps have been described along with the mule deer, but from the hunter's standpoint, this is not practical. The blacktail has its own classification in the Boone and Crockett Club records. It also lives in a different type of habitat than the mule deer, so hunting techniques are different. The black-tailed deer looks very much like the mule deer except that it is generally smaller in body and antler size. The average blacktail buck weighs about 125 pounds with does weighing little less. They only other difference between it and the mule deer is the black bushy tail which is larger than the tail of the mule deer. It is, of course, this tail that gives the black-tailed deer its name.

The range of the blacktail runs from the coast of southern Alaska down to the coast of central California. Blacktails rarely go east of the main Rocky Mountain range.

Hunting Hints — The blacktail can be hunted by the same techniques used for the whitetail. Still hunting at a slow pace is the best bet. The idea is not to venture deep into the Pacific coast rain forest if at all possible because the cover is so thick that getting a shot is very difficult. The hunter should remain near openings — meadows, logged over areas, and old logging roads. The edges of these areas frequently have shrubs and young trees. The blacktails come out to browse during the early mornings and later afternoons. Taking a stand on a deer trail also has good possibilities. A good rifle for whitetails is also good for blacktails because both are hunted in thick cover.

Oregon and Washington both have good blacktail hunting in some areas, but no doubt British Columbia and Alaska are the best. The northern portion of Vancouver Island, British Columbia, is a good place to bag a blacktail and is reasonably accessible. The remote coastal areas of British Columbia and Alaska are, of course, even better, but harder to reach.

THE ELK   *Cervus canadensis*

A bull elk in his prime is a regal animal. His antlers rank as a trophy that few other big game species can equal, but not really surpass. The name "elk" is something of a misnomer. The animal was named by the early colonists after the elk of Europe, but the European elk is in reality the animal we call moose. The European red deer, *Cervus europus*, is a close cousin of the North American elk. A more correct term for our elk is "wapiti", a name of Shawnee Indian origin. This name has never gained wide acceptance.

The elk is an animal of the wilderness. At one time it even existed in the eastern woodlands. Today it is found from the interior of central British Columbia and western Alberta south through the western mountains to

New Mexico and Arizona. It is also found in the coastal range of California, Oregon, Washington, and southern British Columbia. The tule elk of California is a subspecies of *Cervus canadensis*. It is endangered and fully protected. Elk are also found in the forests of Saskatchewan and Manitoba. There are additional small isolated herds in many other states, including Afongank Island in Alaska.

A mature bull elk is an animal generally weighing from 700 to 1000 pounds. The cows run about three-quarters this size.

Hunting Hints — When disturbed by human activity, elk move out by the fastest route available to an area many miles away. Consequently it is

16. Elks must rate as one of this continent's finest trophies. It is a member of the deer family and has a wide distribution ranging from Alaska to Arizona.

17. Big game hunting in the west frequently requires a pack horse trip into the mountains and forests. The trip itself contributes a great deal to making a western hunt a memorable experience.

important to keep noise to a minimum when camping out in elk country. A hunt for elk frequently requires a pack-in trip with a string of horses. Riding through the mountain and forest trails contributes to making an elk hunt a memorable experience. Mule deer are frequently a side trophy on an elk hunt.

One of the best ways to hunt elk is by "bugling". The hunter imitates the bugle of an elk on a bamboo bugle hoping to get an answer. The best time to bugle is on clear frosty mornings. The best places to bugle are high ridges, canyon rims, and large open meadows. When an elk answers, the hunter then carefully stalks the animal hoping to get a shot.

Another way to hunt elk is by stalking on horseback. This requires glassing of all terrain carefully, hoping to locate a good bull. Elk are less disturbed by horses on their range than by men on foot. When a bull has been located, the final stalk is made on foot so that the hunter is ready for a shot. Elk are extremely wary. They have outstanding senses of hearing and smell. A hunter must be quiet at all times and keep the wind in his favor. Because of the noise factor, hunting elk in heavy forest is difficult — a real challenge for a master woodsman. Once an elk has been spooked, he generally clears out — not like a deer which will slip out and be back in the same general area the following day.

A bull elk is a big tough animal requiring a rifle of at least .270 or 7 mm caliber, but the more powerful .30 calibers such as the .30,06 and the various .300 magnums are probably even better.

All the states and provinces in the elk's main range have elk seasons. However, Wyoming, Montana, and Idaho are generally the best bet for elk, particularly for the non-resident because many excellent outfitters operate, specializing in elk hunts. The interior of southern British Columbia also has excellent elk hunting and fine outfitters.

THE MOOSE   *Alces alces*

The moose is an animal of the northern forests with their characteristic heavy snowfalls. It is circumpolar in distribution, thus it is found in northern Europe and Asia as well as North America. The animal gets its name from an Indian word. In Europe, it is known as an elk.

The range of the moose extends from Newfoundland (where it was introduced) westward through the forests of Canada right to the Rockies and from there north throughout Alaska, the Yukon, and the Northwest Territories. Southward it ranges through the mountain forests of Idaho, Montana, and Wyoming. Northern Minnesota has a growing moose herd, and recently held a short open season. The wilderness areas of Maine also have moose.

The average bull moose weighs about 900 to 1400 pounds, but weights of up to 1800 pounds have been recorded. Cows generally run from 700 to 900 pounds.

Hunting Hints — One of the most thrilling ways to hunt moose is to call them during the rut. The hunter, but more likely his guide, bellows like a rival bull or a cow in heat to attract a bull. This is not easy. The bull may or may not come to the call and if he does, he may sneak in as quietly as a ghost to look over the situation or come roaring in like a tank. Calling moose is a favorite hunting method in Ontario and Quebec. Dusk or dawn

18. The moose is also a member of the deer family. It is a stately animal, with some bulls sporting tremendous racks. Alaska, the Yukon, the Northwest Territories, northern Alberta, and Newfoundland are the best places to bag a moose.

are good times to call on shores of lakes with the hunter paddling quietly in a canoe.

Stalking moose is a good technique in the more open areas such as meadows, open muskeg, and stands of short willows of the west or northwest, or on large cutovers, forest fire burns, and the muskeg of the east. The hunter walks or rides on horseback through the interspersed forests and meadows glassing the countryside with his binoculars. When a bull moose is spotted, the hunter attempts to stalk it.

19. *In the forests of eastern Canada — Manitoba, Ontario, and Quebec — moose are frequently called up during the rutting season. The bull, if he comes, may approach as silently as a ghost or may come roaring in like a locomotive.*

During the early season moose feed on aquatic vegetation in marshes and the shallows of lakes. For this reason, in Manitoba, Ontario, and Quebec, a canoe is frequently an important piece of the moose hunter's equipment. It allows the hunter to cover vast areas quickly and quietly.

In areas where the season is open when the snow is on the ground, another good technique is to track moose on snowshoes. This is a hard and thrilling way to hunt moose for someone who has the physical endurance and is a good hunter. In winter moose frequently feed by breaking down saplings a few inches thick. They break these by rearing on them with their chests and then browsing on the tender twigs. A moose breaking down saplings can be heard for long distances; the sound of a breaking sapling in the frosty air is like the crack of a pistol. A hunter should listen for this. I have shot a number of moose which I first heard feeding and then carefully stalked upwind.

A good elk rifle generally makes a good moose rifle.

The "rack" of a bull moose is one of our finest trophies. The Boone and Crockett Club divides moose into three divisions because of the variation in size of racks. The biggest racks come from the Alaska-Yukon moose, the next largest from the Canada moose found throughout the forests of Canada from British Columbia to Newfoundland, and the smallest racks come from the smallest race of moose, the Wyoming or Shiras moose of the western United States. A record book bull moose can occur just about anywhere in its range.

Alaska, the Yukon, and the Northwest Territories are three top areas for moose hunting. Northern Alberta has one of the densest moose herds per square mile on the continent, as has Newfoundland. Good moose hunting also exists in parts of Quebec, Ontario, Manitoba, Saskatchewan, and British Columbia. In Canada, the number of moose licenses available outnumbers the hunters. There are no special draw permits.

THE CARIBOU   *Rangifer tarandus*

In autumn, when the antlers are shiny, clear of velvet, and the sleek winter coat has fully grown, the adult caribou bull is a striking animal. The caribou's range extends from Newfoundland through northern Quebec, around Hudson Bay to British Columbia, north through Alaska and the Northwest Territories including many of the arctic islands and coastal areas of Greenland. In the mountain country of the west, caribou are found almost as far south as the U.S. — Canada border at Idaho.

At one time it was believed that there were several species of caribou in North America. However, only one species is recognized today, with several geographic races. The caribou of these races differ somewhat in size, color of hide, and shape and size of antlers. The woodland caribou is the biggest, while those of the arctic islands are generally the smallest. The caribou of North America and the reindeer of Europe are the same animal. The caribou bulls vary in size from as much as 400 pounds for the woodland race to 150 pounds for the Arctic race. The cows are a little smaller.

Hunting Hints — Caribou have good senses of hearing and smell, but their eyesight is relatively poor. They are also somewhat curious. The best technique for hunting them is walking or riding the rolling hilltops and ridges, glassing the countryside below. In Newfoundland, hunters walk through the forest and glass the flat stretches of muskeg "barrens". When a good bull is spotted, the stalk is made keeping the wind in favor. The stalk can be difficult or easy depending on the terrain and cover, and even the wariness of individual animals. Woodland caribou when hunted in forests are more elusive.

Generally caribou are not too difficult to hunt. They are not particularly wary. However, the great shovelled antlers of the bulls make an impressive trophy and caribou meat is probably the best venison of all. It certainly is superior to the meat of deer or elk.

Any moderately powerful rifle from a .25,06 to a .300 magnum, preferably with a 'scope sight of moderate power, is a suitable weapon for caribou.

For the Boone and Crockett Club trophy records, caribou are divided into mountain, woodland, barren ground, and Quebec-Labrador classes. For barren ground caribou, Alaska is hard to beat, although good racks are taken in the Yukon and the Northwest Territories. Top mountain caribou racks come from British Columbia, but Alberta also has some fine caribou hunting. The woodland caribou comes from Newfoundland and, as the name indicates, the Quebec-Labrador race comes from this region.

THE PRONGHORN ANTELOPE *Antilocapra americana*

The pronghorn antelope is strictly a North American animal. It is unique, with no close relatives anywhere in the world. The name antelope is biologically incorrect, because the animal is not an antelope. It should more accurately be called simply "pronghorn". The bucks weigh 100 to 125 pounds while the does are slightly smaller.

Hunting Hints — The pronghorn's eyesight is remarkable. It is also one of the fastest animals in the world, being capable of running 60 miles per hour. These two attributes make the pronghorn a difficult animal to hunt. The best technique is to glass the plains with powerful binoculars from high ridges. When a good buck is spotted, the hunter then tries to stalk it using all available cover and any gulllies and ravines. Stalking the pronghorn requires a great deal of stealth because in every herd two or three animals are always on the lookout.

Pronghorns are generally shot at long ranges. A high velocity cartridge with a flat trajectory is needed. Anything from a .243 or 6 mm to a .300 magnum is a good choice. Calibers such as the .25,06, .270, and 7 mm magnum are probably the best bets. The rifle must be very accurate and scoped with a sight of at least 4 power, with some hunters preferring 6 power.

Wyoming is undoubtedly the best pronghorn state, but eastern Montana is also good. Other states and provinces also have pronghorn seasons, but in some cases they are restricted to residents only.

THE BIGHORN SHEEP   *Ovis canadensis*

The bighorn sheep, with its heavy curling horns, is a spectacular animal. It is our most coveted trophy. Yet I can't help but wonder if it's not the grandeur of the mountains that contribute to making the sheep such a beautiful animal. The mountain country is as beautiful as the sheep. However, without the sheep, the mountains would seem barren.

Bighorns are divided into two classes by the Boone and Crockett Club — the Rocky Mountain bighorn and the desert bighorn.

The range of the bighorns extends from central British Columbia and Alberta south through the western mountains into northern Mexico and Baja California. The arid hills of Nevada, California, New Mexico, Arizona, and Mexico are the habitat of the desert bighorns. Desert bighorns are less numerous than mountain bighorns.

Both male and female bighorns have horns, but those of the ewes are smaller, lighter, and never complete a "curl". Mature bighorn rams may weigh up to 300 pounds, but 250 is a more usual weight. The ewes are about three-quarters this size.

Hunting Hints — A sheep hunt is an exhilarating experience. The bighorns have exceptionally keen eyesight, which some hunters rate equal to that of a man with 8-power binoculars. This is their chief line of defense for detecting enemies. Their hearing and sense of smell, however, are also very good.

The usual way to hunt sheep is a pack-in trip into the mountains on horseback. But in some areas, particularly in desert bighorn country, it is possible to drive with four-wheel drive vehicles close enough to the mountains to begin hunting. Sheep hunting involves climbing and a great deal of walking. A hunter must be in good physical shape. Generally sheep do not live in quite as rugged a habitat or as high up as mountain goats.

The best tactic for sheep hunting is climbing onto high vantage points and glassing the countryside for sheep. Bighorns, being brown, blend in well with the terrain. Good binoculars are a must. In fact, experienced sheep hunters believe that good binoculars are more important for sheep hunting than the 'scope on a rifle. When sheep are sighted, a spotting 'scope is used to determine their sex and evaluate their horns.

Once a trophy ram is sighted, the stalk begins. To qualify as a trophy, the horns of the ram must form at least three-quarters curl. The ideal way to stalk a sheep is to get above it and work down to within good rifle range.

20. The bighorn sheep is considered by many hunters to be this continent's finest big game trophy. Only the white Dall sheep of Alaska and the Yukon can match it. The ram on the lower left has a fine head.

Sheep rarely look up the mountains for danger. Their natural enemies, wolves and cougars, always approach from below. A sheep rifle should be flat shooting, moderately powerful, and equipped with a moderate power 'scope, 4 power being ideal. Anything from a .25 caliber such as the .25,06 up to the .300 magnum is a good bet. The rifle should also be fairly light and relatively short-barrelled so that it is easy to carry. A good guide is a must for sheep hunting.

The best place to get a Rocky Mountain bighorn is in the mountains of southwestern Alberta and in the East Kootenays of British Columbia, western Montana, and the Salmon River drainage of Idaho. Wyoming also offers some special draw permits to non-residents. Sheep hunting in Utah, Oregon, Colorado and Washington is generally limited to residents only. Getting a license for a desert bighorn is difficult. New Mexico, Arizona, and Nevada all have very limited seasons, but only New Mexico and Arizona allow a few permits for non-residents. Occasionally a few sheep permits are allowed in Mexico.

THE DALL SHEEP   *Ovis dalli*

The Dall, along with its subspecies the Fannin and Stone, is a sheep of the northern mountains. The Dall is the most northerly of the three, with the Fannin and Stone races being found farther south. These sheep differ from the bighorn in the shape of their horns and the color of their coats. The coat of the Dall is white and its horns are thinner in structure and flare out at the tips. Because of this, the Dall is sometimes called the "thinhorn".

The snow white Dall vies with the bighorn as North America's top trophy. The Stone sheep is dark grey to almost black in color and its horns are somewhat bigger than that of the Dall. For this reason it has a classification of its own in the Boone and Crockett Club records.

The range of the Dall sheep extends from northern Alaska through the MacKenzie Mountains of the Yukon and the Northwest Territories as far south as northern British Columbia.

Hunting Hints — Hunting for Dall sheep essentially involves the same techniques as hunting for bighorns, except that it is usually done in even more remote and rugged areas. The Dall sheep is hard to see on a background of snow which can come early in the far north. However, in the early season, the white coat of the Dall stands out well against the green alpine meadows and grey-brown rocks.

The best place to bag a Dall sheep is in the mountains of Alaska and the Yukon, the Northwest Territories, and the northwest corner of British Columbia. The Stone and Fannin sheep are found in the northern part of British Columbia and the southeast Yukon.

THE MOUNTAIN GOAT   *Oreamnos americanus*

The mountain goat, not really a goat, is actually related to the antelopes of Asia and Africa. It does, however, look and act a little like a goat. It lives in the mountains like a goat, so logically enough it was named mountain goat by the first white men who saw it.

The mountain goat's range extends from the high mountain peaks of southern Alaska, the Yukon, and the Northwest Territories south through British Columbia and Alberta into Washington, Montana, and Idaho.

131

Mountain goats are also found in small herds in Wyoming and the Black Hills of South Dakota.

The mountain goat is a striking white animal. It is a mountain climber of such capability that no mountain slope seems to be beyond its range. The males or billies weigh 200 to 300 pounds. The females are slightly smaller. Both sexes have horns, with those of the female frequently being longer, but those of the male are thicker and more massive.

Hunting Hints — The hunter who is interested in a mountain goat trophy must be in top physical condition and must not be afraid of heights.

21. The mountain goat lives in the high peaks of the western mountains. A hunter who wants to bag one has to be in good physical shape and must not be afraid of heights. British Columbia is the best place to bag a goat.

Mountain goat hunting is for the tough and adventurous. Usually it involves horse pack-trips into mountain caps from where the peaks are scaled.

Good binoculars and a spotting 'scope are invaluable. The hunters walk or sometimes ride on sure-footed mountain horses and glass the mountain sides for goats. When the animals are sighted, the spotting 'scope is used to evaluate and examine the animals to see if they are mature trophy billies.

When a good billy is spotted, the stalk begins, frequently involving much climbing. Sometimes the stalk has to be abandoned because the goat is in an inaccessible place. Before shooting, always make certain that after the shot the goat cannot fall down a mountain side to be lost or smashed up.

The rifle for goat hunting should be light and accurate. It should be chambered for a cartridge with a flat trajectory. Cartridges from .270 to .300 magnum are good choices. The ideal sight is a mid-powered 'scope.

British Columbia is undoubtedly the best goat country. All of the major mountain ranges have goats. Southern Alaska and Yukon run second. Nearly all the top heads in the Boone and Crockett Club records come from these three places. Incidentally, any horns over 10 inches in length and 5½ inches in circumference at the base are almost certain to make the book.

THE JAVELINA
Tayassu tajacu

The javelina is a pig-like animal of the dry brushy and scrub oak forests of the southwestern United States and Mexico. The proper name of the animal is the collared peccary; the animal is, however, better known by its Spanish title of javelina, derived from its javelin-like tusks.

The javelina stands about 22 inches high at the shoulder and weighs 40 to 65 pounds. Its body is covered with coarse, bristly hair that is "salt and pepper" in color. The javelina has a musk gland on its back which can emit a strong and unpleasant odor in alarm or anger.

The range of the javelina extends from southwestern Texas, southern New Mexico, and southern Arizona southward to Mexico.

Hunting Hints — Javelina seasons tend to be short and hunting permits are not all that plentiful. They are sometimes available only on a special draw basis. So the wise hunter scouts the country first, even before the season opens, looking for fresh signs such as tracks and droppings. If a hunter can locate a water hole that the little desert pigs are using, so much the better.

Javelinas can be hunted in a manner similar to deer. The hunter can watch a water hole that the pigs are using. This is a pastime for the patient man.

Still hunting is probably the most appealing and perhaps the most productive technique. The hunter must move slowly on the edges of brush patches and scrub forests. The pigs must be surprised in the open. Getting a shot in the brush is almost impossible. Since javelinas always travel in

133

22. The javelina, more properly called the collared peccary, is a small pig-like animal of the southwest. The brush country of southern Texas and northern Mexico are the places to bag one of these desert pigs, but New Mexico and Arizona also have short seasons.

herds, getting close to them is not easy. One or two animals are constantly fully alert, scenting and listening for danger. When the hunter actually spots a band of javelinas, he must plan his stalk very carefully by staying away from brush where walking is noisy.

A hunter must keep the wind in his favor at all times. By hunting upwind, the hunter might pick up the scent of javelinas before he actually sees the pigs. Hunters have come across bands of javelinas lying up in thick cover without actually seeing the animals. They suddenly appear on all sides, racing away in different directions.

Javelinas have also been hunted with dogs. A well trained dog pack will single out one animal and bring it to bay. Dogs have no trouble bringing a javelina to bay. The pig has speed, but no endurance. The dogs must learn to keep away from the sharp tusks. Dogs have been killed by cornered javelinas. Once a javelina has been bayed, the hunter can generally approach it for a close shot.

I doubt if many dog packs are kept for the purpose of hunting these desert pigs — perhaps none at all. Hunting the peccary with dogs is not legal everywhere, and the hunting seasons are too short to train dogs properly.

How good are javelinas to eat? Now here's a question that's good for an argument any time. Young piglets are generally regarded as very tasty. The meat of adult boars tends to be dry. If the animal has not been dressed out properly with the musk glands removed immediately after shooting, the meat can be unpalatable. Smoked javelina is said to be very good, while other hunters prefer it barbecued.

Almost any rifle from a .243 to a 6 or 7 mm and up is suitable for javelina. When open shooting is most likely, a flat shooting cartridge is the best choice. For very brushy country, the old .30-30 is as good as anything.

The best place to bag a javelina is in Texas with Val Verde, Terrell, and Pecos counties being the best bet. Southeastern Arizona also has fairly good desert pig hunting generally by special draw in Pima, Cochise, Santa Cruz, and Graham counties. New Mexico also has a short javelina season by special draw in Hidalgo county. There are also many areas of Mexico where javelinas are abundant and the hunting seasons are long.

THE WILD BOAR   *Sus scrofa*

The wild boar is native to Europe and Asia where it is simultaneously prized as a big game animal and regarded as something of a menace to agriculture. Certainly a family herd of wild pigs can cause a tremendous amount of damage to a grain or potato field in a single night. The domestic hog is a descendant of the wild boar.

Wild pigs on this continent come from two stocks. Genuine wild boars were trapped in Germany and Russia and brought to hunting preserves in the Blue Mountains of New Hampshire, the Adirondacks of New York, the Great Smokies of Tennessee, Hooper's Bald of North Carolina, and to several areas of California during the first quarter of this century.

The second stock is from domestic hogs gone wild — feral hogs. This is the famous razorback of Florida and North Carolina. This is also the wild pig of Hawaii. In North Carolina the native razorback and the wild boar have interbred.

The wild pigs look very much like the domestic hog. The true wild boar

135

is black with long black or dark bristly hair. The hair on the back and shoulders is longer than elsewhere. In the males, the canine teeth turn upward and form formidable tusks, up to 9 inches in length. The ears of the true wild boar tend to be erect, but those of the razorback may be drooping. The razorback is also generally lighter in color and its hair is not as long as that of the wild boar. The wild pigs may grow up to 400 pounds, but a 300-pounder is generally a good size, and razorbacks may be smaller. Wild pigs never get fat.

Hunting Hints — The hound chase is the most exciting way to hunt wild pigs. It is not as popular as it used to be, but it is still practiced in North Carolina and Tennessee. Razorbacks are also hunted in Florida with dogs.

The method is similar to bear hunting with hounds. Hunters are posted in spots where the boars might cross ahead of the dogs. Then a hunter takes the pack through. When the dogs hit a fresh track, the chase is on. The boar may cross near a hunter, giving the hunter a shot. The hounds may also bring the boar to bay. When this happens, the hunters try to approach the boar upwind to get a shot before the boar mangles one of the dogs.

The boar chase can take a long time and can go a long distance. Dogs have been known to stay on an old boar's trail for days, never bringing it to bay. The boar chase is a sport for the tough and hardy. It also requires experienced dogs who know how to stay away from the boar's tusks.

In Florida the razorbacks are not always shot. When the dogs have brought the hog to bay, special "catch" dogs grab the animal and the hunters sneak in to catch the pig. Sometimes the hunters ride horses. The pigs are then penned up and fattened before being slaughtered. Catching wild hogs is a pastime for adventurous souls.

Still hunting is the most common way of hunting wild pigs. The hunter walks slowly, stopping frequently to look and listen. It goes without saying that the hunter should concentrate his efforts in areas where there are plenty of signs — tracks, droppings, fresh mud wallows, and signs of pigs rooting in the earth for mast, roots, or tubers.

It is important that the hunter always hunt with the wind in his favor. Wild pigs have a very keen sense of smell and sharp hearing. They tend to be most active at dawn and dusk. In Hawaii, wild pigs tend to live in very thick cover where they are hard to hunt. The only way to bag one is while they are out feeding in the open during the early morning or evening hours. Any good deer rifle would be suitable for wild boars. Calibers from .270 and up would be the best bet.

Wild boars are not plentiful anywhere. They are gone from New York, and probably New Hampshire. They never received any protection in these two states because they caused agricultural damage. In the south, they are largely confined to non-farming areas — the mountain or bush country.

Both Tennessee and North Carolina have short seasons on wild boars. In California, there is a season in Monterey county. In the rest of the state they can be hunted at any time because they cause agricultural damage. Hawaii has open seasons on the razorback as does Florida. Hawaii has the best wild pig hunting, with Florida coming second.

THE BLACK BEAR   *Ursus americanus*

The black bear is the most abundant and widely distributed of all the bears in North America. His cousins, the polar bear and the grizzly, are also found in Asia and northern Europe. The black bear is a very adaptable animal. It can live close to human settlement.

23. The black bear is our most widely distributed bear. Its range extends from Florida to Alaska. This is one big game species that can be hunted even by a man of moderate financial means.

The range of the black bear extends from Newfoundland west through most of Canada and south through New England and the Appalachian Mountains. Its western range extends from Alaska and the Yukon south along the coast into California and through the western mountains into northern Mexico. Some bears still hang on in Florida.

The black bear is not, as one might suspect, always black. The western races can be brown or cinnamon in color, and one race known as the "glacier" bear is almost blue. Adult bears run to about 350 pounds, but 500-pound animals have been shot. Sows are generally slightly smaller than boars.

Hunting Hints — The black bear is a very intelligent animal with a good sense of smell and hearing. It is not an easy animal to hunt. A good time to hunt black bears is in spring shortly after the bears have emerged from their winter dormancy and are still feeding on fresh grass. The hunter should watch over forest and mountain meadows which have luxurious growths of fresh grass.

Later, when the bears have started feeding on carrion, the best way to hunt them is to set a bait of slaughterhouse offal or fish in areas frequented by bears. The baits should be placed so that the hunter can watch over them from a good vantage point. This is not the most challenging or the most exciting way to hunt the bruin, but it is not all that easy. In Alaska and British Columbia, a good way to hunt black bears is along rivers that have heavy runs of salmon where the bears are known to fish.

In the west, black bears are taken as a side trophy on hunts for other big game. They are usually glassed on the alpine meadows and stalked. Through the east, in New England, Quebec, Ontario, and Manitoba, many bears are also bagged by moose and deer hunters.

Black bears are also hunted with hounds in the southern United States, in Michigan, and even in Washington and Oregon, but not in Canada. This is perhaps the most exciting way to hunt bears.

The technique for hunting black bears with hounds is simple, but actually bagging a bear is difficult. The hound pack is taken through good bear country. When the dogs find fresh scent, they immediately take after the bear. The hunters are posted throughout the area, with the hope that the bear will pass within shooting range of one of the hunters. Frequently the hounds bring the bear to bay in some thick cover against a rocky outcrop. The hunters must then go in and kill the bear before one of the hounds is mauled or the bear takes the hounds on another chase.

Bear hounds can be of any large breed — Walkers, blue-ticks, Plotts, redbones, black and tans, or even mixed breeds. They must, however, be fully broken of chasing "trash" — deer, foxes, or any other animal. Each pack must have dogs with "cold noses" to pick up cold scents and "catch" or "strike" dogs that will actually bring a bear to bay and hold it there so that the hunters can approach.

A good black bear rifle is also one that is used for white-tailed deer or other big game. Incidentally, the meat of a black bear that has been feeding on acorns and beechnuts is quite good.

The most dense black bear populations occur in areas of coastal Alaska and British Columbia. These are the best areas to bag a black bear. But not everyone can afford to make such a trip. Washington is also good bear country, but a hunter can bag a bear while after other game almost anywhere in the bruin's range. In the east, the best place to bag a bear is northern Ontario and Quebec. There are a fair number of outfitters who specialize in spring bear hunts in these two provinces.

THE GRIZZLY AND ALASKA BROWN BEARS   *Ursus arctos*

At one time the Alaska brown bear and the grizzly were regarded as separate species. Modern biologists have conclusively proven that outside of size, there is no biological difference between these two big bears.

> *24. The grizzly is an animal of the western wilderness. Its unpredict-ability and at times its aggressive nature have confined it to that. Few hunters realize that the grizzly and the Alaska brown bear are the same species.*

The big bears are animals of the wilderness. Their unpredictable nature has consigned them to that. Unfortunately, there is little place for large and occasionally aggressive animals near human settlement. Because of this, the range of these big bears is decreasing. The bears are not in danger of extinction. There is still a vast tract of wilderness left in Alaska and Canada, but we must not be complacent about the big bears' future. Man, in his never-ending quest for minerals, petroleum, and timber, is penetrating and subduing the wilderness. We must halt some of this frenzy before the wilderness disappears, and the big bears with it.

The range of the Alaska brown bear extends along the coast of southern Alaska including, of course, Kodiak Island which is famous for its big bears. The grizzly ranges from the mountains of Wyoming, Montana, and Idaho north through British Columbia and western Alberta, and through the western part of the Northwest Territories, the Yukon, and the interior of Alaska.

The grizzly is an inland bear. It weighs 500 to 800 pounds, with the females generally running 400 to 600 pounds. The main reason for the size difference between the Alaska brown and the grizzly is diet. The Alaska brown is a coastal animal with fish — salmon — forming an important part of its diet. Fish are very rich in proteins and oils. Because the grizzly is an inland bear, food is not as abundant or of as high a quality. Thus the grizzly is smaller and rangier.

The Alaska brown bear vies with the polar bear for the title of the world's largest carnivore. Big males weigh between 800 and 1200 pounds, with even larger bears having been recorded. Females generally weigh 500 to 800 pounds.

The pelts of these big bears vary in color from dark brown to almost blond or russet. The interior bears frequently have white-tipped guard hairs, a sort of frosting.

Hunting Hints — Spring is also the best time to hunt big bears. Bear pelts at this time are rich and glossy with no patches of hair rubbed out. The bears can be hunted as they feed on green grass in mountain meadows. However, most grizzlies are shot by hunters who pack into the mountains on big game hunts with strings of pack horses. This hunting technique consists of glassing the meadows for bears out feeding on berries, digging out marmots and ground squirrels, or just wandering about. Baits, in the form of offal from elk and moose kills, are also sometimes used. The grizzlies at this time of year are foraging for food almost continuously to store up fat for the winter. In areas where there are good fall salmon runs, the bears are hunted by watching stretches of streams. The big browns are frequently hunted from boats.

Once a bear is sighted and appears to be a big lone animal, indicating a mature bear, the hunter attemps to stalk the animal to within good rifle range. It is important to be quiet and work upwind. The grizzly has good hearing and a keen sense of smell.

A rifle for grizzlies should be reasonably powerful, certainly nothing under .270 is adequate and the various .30 caliber cartridges from .30,06 and up are a better bet. Even the .338, .35 Remington or Norma magnums and the .375 magnum calibers are not too much of a rifle for the big bears, particularly the Alaska browns, if the hunter can shoot them accurately. A wounded grizzly in thick cover is nothing to fool with. Many guides and hunters have been mauled and even killed by wounded grizzlies and Alaska browns. Get close and shoot straight is the best advice I can give you.

Northern British Columbia, the Northwest Territories, the Yukon, and the interior of Alaska are the best places to bag a grizzly. The southern Alaska coast is the only area for the big browns. A hunter who wants a big bear more than any other trophy should book with an outfitter whose clients have a high success rate on the big bears. This is as good an indication as any that the outfitter is operating in an area that has an abundance of bears and that his guides know how to hunt them.

Incidentally, it is the skulls of bears, not the skins, that are used to rank them in the Boone and Crockett Club trophy records.

THE POLAR BEAR   *Ursus maritimus*

The polar bear is a magnificent animal of the snow, ice, and water of the arctic. It is equally at home in water as on the masses of ice many feet thick, or on land. Outside of man, the "ice" bear's only enemy is the killer whale which on rare occasions kills a swimming bear.

The polar bear is circumpolar. It is found around the entire fringe of the arctic circle. In North America it is found around the entire arctic coast line including Greenland, the arctic islands, and wanders occasionally as far south as James Bay in Ontario.

The polar bear is generally heavier than the brown bear of the Alaskan coast. White bears of 1600 pounds have been shot, but the average is around 1000 pounds.

Hunting Hints — With the enactment of the Marine Mammal Protection Act, polar bear became protected from hunting in the territories of the United States. The only exception is that native people living in the traditional manner may still hunt the bear. The reason for this ban is the possibility that polar bear populations have decreased rapidly. However, no one can say if the decrease has been drastic enough to threaten the polar bear's survival. No one knows how many polar bears exist in the world, because they are almost impossible to census. Polar bears roam about constantly and over great distances.

There can be no doubt that hunting the ice bears by spotting them from aircraft was responsible for the decrease of bears off the coast of Alaska. We hunters have to share the blame for allowing these bears to be hunted

141

25. *The polar bear is a magnificent animal of the ice and snow.*
Hunting the "great ice bear" is prohibited in United States territory
under the Marine Mammal Protection Act.

in such a manner. Such hunting offered little or no challenge. It was not "fair chase" and for this reason the Boone and Crockett Club refused to accept polar bear skulls for trophy competition. Polar bear hunting by spotting the animals from aircraft was a big business. It owed its existence to "quick buck" operators and hunters with low sporting ethics. If I sound bitter about this unholy episode, it's because I am. It has blackened the name of all hunting and hunters. It also means that many hunters — the real hunters — who would have been more than happy to hunt the white bear in the traditional way with dog sleds can no longer do so. Chances are that the polar bear will never appear on the open season list. Once a game animal has been taken off, it is very hard to put it back.

The aircraft hunters were not the only ones that helped to reduce the polar bear population. Until very recently commercial hunting of ice bears was allowed in Norwegian territories. I have heard many stories of large numbers of bears being shot, including the practice of taking bears by baited "set guns".

The only place where the polar bear can still be hunted by white sportsmen is in the Northwest Territories where the Eskimo villages at Sachs Harbour on Banks Island and Resolute Bay on Cornwallis Island provide outfitting services for polar bear hunters. Unfortunately the Marine Mammal Protection Act also bans the importation of all products made of marine mammals. This means that an American sportsman going on such a polar bear hunt could not bring his trophy back into the United States.

Eskimos are allowed to hunt polar bears for meat and skin. Each village is allowed a quota of bears. In the case of Sachs Harbour and Resolute Bay, outside hunters are allowed to shoot five bears per year out of each village, one bear per hunter, from the village quotas. The hunter also has to purchase a territorial polar bear license for $250. The hunter keeps the skin and skull for trophy, and the village gets the meat.

The hunts are carried on in the traditional manner with sled dogs. The hunters and their guides strike across the ice until they find a fresh track. The track is then followed until the bear is sighted. The hunter stalks the bear or tries to get ahead of the bear and waits for it, depending on whichever is more feasible. The guide may also release his dogs to bring the bear to bay so that the hunter can approach for a shot. The cost of such a hunt is $3000. Arrangements are made through the Game Department at Yellowknife.

Hunting polar bears in this manner is sport for big game hunters who want to experience maximum thrills and danger. It is not for the physically frail and soft. The polar bear is not afraid of man. It recognizes no enemy. A rifle for the polar bear should be the same as for grizzlies. Both bears are tough adversaries.

THE COUGAR   *Felis concolor*
The cougar, frequently referred to as the puma or mountain lion, is an animal of the wilderness. Its predation on livestock makes it unwelcome in farming or ranching country. For this reason, bounties were at one time placed on its head and this beautiful cat was persecuted the year around. Only recently have we become intelligent enough to slowly recognize the cougar as an outstanding big game animal.

At one time it was distributed over much of North America's forests, including the eastern woodlands. Now its main range exists from central British Columbia including Vancouver Island and central Alberta south through the western forests into South America. All of the western and southwestern states have cougars. The cat still exists in small numbers in Louisiana and Florida. There is also some evidence to indicate that the eastern race of cougars is not extinct. Sightings of the cat are regularly reported in New Brunswick and occasionally in Maine.

A male cougar can weigh up to 175 pounds, with larger specimens having been shot. The females weigh only about 60 percent of that.

Hunting Hints — The most successful, and indeed about the only way to hunt cougars is with hounds. The hunter takes his hound pack into the mountains or wilderness and looks for fresh signs — tracks or a kill. The hounds are then released to follow the cat.

Cougars fear dogs. They can run fast, but they do not have the stamina required for long distance running. The cougar tries to escape by going into rough country where the dogs cannot follow. If this does not shake the dogs, the hounds eventually bring the cat to bay on a rocky ledge or in a tree. The hunter follows the baying hounds on horseback if possible, and on foot if necessary. When the pack has treed the cat, it is shot or let go for another day. It is the hound chase that makes cougar hunting so exciting.

There is probably no single top place to hunt cougars. British Columbia probably has the densest population of them, mainly because it has a dense deer population. But such states as Idaho, Montana, and Wyoming are good bets. Washington and Oregon are also good. The wilderness areas of New Mexico and Arizona have good cougar populations. The success of the cougar hunt depends far more on the reliability of the guide and his hounds than on the hunter. Generally speaking, guides who specialize in cougar hunting live in or near good mountain lion country.

The cougar is an outstanding big game animal. It is unfortunate that a few states still classify it as a varmint to be destroyed on sight. The blame for this can be placed on a hard core of influential cattlemen. It would be better to repay ranchers for any livestock lost to cougars than to have the animals branded as varmints.

THE WOLVES
                                                    Canis spp.

There are two species of wolves in North America — the gray wolf *(Canis lupus)* which in Canada is called the timber wolf, and the red wolf *(Canis niger)*. The red wolf today is very rare and is considered endangered by most wildlife authorities. Unfortunately little is known about the red wolf. It is mainly found in eastern Texas and western Louisiana, but at one time its range covered the entire Mississippi valley as far north as Illinois. The red wolf is unique to this continent.

144

The gray wolf is circumpolar, being found in northern Europe and northern Asia as well as North America. In North America its range today extends from Labrador through all of northern Canada including the upper peninsula of Michigan and northern Minnesota north to the arctic islands and westward into Alaska. A few pockets of wolves exist in the big national parks in the west and north of Mexico.

Wolves have been feared and hated from time immemorial. There was reason for this fear and hatred in Europe where wolves killed people and were a serious agricultural menace. In North America, seemingly authentic records of wolves attacking humans are rare, and possibly nonexistent. Depredations on livestock, however, were quite common when the first farms and ranches were pushed into the wilderness and wolves were more abundant. Today, wildlife scientists have proven that wolf predations on game animals are not as damaging as hunters think, but rather that wolves act as nature's safety valve by culling the old and less able and keeping the game herds within the carrying capacity of the range.

The gray wolf looks like a large German shepherd dog. Its pelt can vary in color from almost coal black to almost white but grey is the most common. An adult male timber wolf of the arctic races can weigh up to 175 pounds, but the normal weight is 80 to 100 pounds. The females are generally about 20 percent smaller.

The red wolf is smaller than the gray or timber wolf. Its color is predominantly tawny with black on the back. Other than this difference in coloration and size, the red wolf looks very much like the gray wolf.

Hunting Hints — About the only way to hunt wolves is to meander in areas where they live and watch. The key word is watch. Good binoculars are a must. This hunting technique is only really successful in the more open country of the western mountains and the north. In the eastern forests, a hunter who knows which beaver meadows and lakeshores the wolves are frequenting might have a chance to bag one.

Wolves can also be hunted by stalking a pack whose location is revealed by howling. First, the hunter must locate the home range of the wolf pack. Then he must locate the pack by imitating a wolf howl. When wolves hear another wolf howl, they will frequently respond. When the location of the howling pack is pinpointed, the hunter moves in slowly and quietly upwind. He watches a great deal. This technique works better if two people are involved. One partner keeps howling intermittently while the other attempts to stalk the wolves. I know that this technique works. I have never used it to actually shoot wolves, but I have used it to get close enough to have a good look. Once in Ontario's Algonquin Provincial Park, I got to within about 150 yards of a pack of six wolves using this technique.

In the far north Indians have hunted wolves by snowshoeing after them immediately after a deep, fresh snowfall. This has to be done before a crust forms on the surface. At such times, strong tough men on snowshoes can move along while the wolves flounder. I suspect that few white men would have the physical stamina for this type of hunt.

Today wolves in the open tundra are shot by Indians on snowmobiles, and in Alaska are shot by white men from aircraft. Neither method is sporting. Wolf muscle doesn't stand much of a chance against mechanical horsepower. Fortunately this method of hunting wolves only works in the open tundra. In the forest the wolf still has the advantage. I do not resent Indians using snow machines to hunt wolves, because they are doing it to sell the pelt in a land where jobs are rare and other ways to earn a livelihood are difficult. But I seethe at the thought of an animal being gunned down from an aircraft in our supposedly enlightened age.

The reason I have placed the timber wolf with big game is because this is where this magnificent, highly intelligent animal belongs. It takes a hunter of unusual skill to take a wolf in a fair chase. Any other game animal — bear, moose, sheep, elk, caribou, and even the elusive white-tailed deer — is much easier to shoot. The wolf itself is a hunter of unusual skill and we, as fellow hunters, should have a deep admiration and respect for it.

OTHER NATIVE BIG GAME

There are several other species of big game in North America. The bison *(Bison bison)* is one of these. The buffalo once roamed the prairies in many millions, but wheat fields and fences are not places for buffalo. Today, the biggest herd of buffalo exists in and around the Wood Buffalo National Park in northern Alberta and the Northwest Territories. Smaller herds live in other parks and on private ranches in the United States. The province of Manitoba has two growing herds outside of parks, the largest being north of the town of Ashern in the interlake region.

A limited hunting season is periodically held on the buffalo in the Northwest Territories around the Wood Buffalo National Park. A number of licenses are available for non-residents. The buffalo may also be hunted on some private ranches.

The bison is certainly a spectacular big game animal, but one that offers comparatively little challenge in hunting. The memoirs of some of the buffalo hunters of the old west show this.

The muskox *(Ovibus moschatus)* is another big game animal of the north. This shaggy bovine has, however, until now been fully protected because for a time it was in danger of extinction. The herds have built up, and on some of the Alaskan and arctic islands, muskoxen have become quite numerous, overgrazed their range, and starved in the winter. As this is being written, there are rumors that the Northwest Territories Game Department may allow a limited season. Alaska has also toyed with the thought of a limited season and has set the hunting license at $1000 for non-residents.

In Canada, hunting would be done on a similar basis as the polar bear hunts — through Eskimo villages. Eskimos in Canada's north are allowed a small harvest of muskoxen. I suspect that hunting muskoxen would be much like hunting buffalo.

The walrus (Odobenus rosmarus) is another sea game mammal. But this creature is protected by the same law that bans polar bear hunting. Alaska allowed limited walrus hunting by white hunters. The hunters went out in boats of the ice floes. Once a big bull was spotted, the hunter would stalk the animal. A non-resident license for walrus was $100. Today, only native people may kill the walrus in Alaska. In Canada, the Eskimos have a quota on the number of walruses they may kill for food. Frankly, my view of the walrus as a big game animal places it below the bison or muskox as far as challenge is concerned.

The wolverine (Gulo luscus) is another animal that should be classified as a big game species. A number of states and provinces do so, but others regard it as a varmint. The wolverine has been the subject of many myths of cunnning, ferocity, and evil disposition. Most of these myths are strictly that, with little or no truth behind them.

The wolverine, however, does not hesitate to plunder fur bearing animals from traps. For this reason it is hated by trappers. Wolverine fur is valued by northern residents for trim on parkas because it is oily and does not hoar or frost up when breathed upon in subzero temperatures. The pelt also makes an interesting and seldom encountered trophy. The wolverine is sometimes bagged by big game hunters in Alaska, the Yukon, the Northwest Territories, and northern British Columbia.

EXOTIC BIG GAME

There are a number of exotic species on the open season lists of various states. Texas has the largest number of these exotic species on private ranches. They vary from the mouflon (Ovis musimon), the wild sheep of Europe, to the black buck (Antilope cervicapra), an attractive, fleet-footed animal of India and Pakistan. A number of African antelope and exotic sheep species are also found on Texas ranches. All of these ranches allow hunting for a fee, usually on a "no trophy no fee" basis.

New Mexico has imported the Barbary sheep (Ammotragus lervia), the only wild sheep species found in Africa. The stocking has caught on very well and a limited open season is allowed under a special draw permit. The Barbary sheep of New Mexico are proving to be as difficult to bag as those of north Africa. They are shy, have good eyesight, and are fleet-footed. The Canadian River area of New Mexico is the place to bag this exotic wild sheep. New Mexico has also imported other exotic big game species, including some of the African desert antelope.

Hawaii has the largest variety of exotic big game. Indeed, all big game in

26. *The Barbary sheep, a native of northern Africa, has been introduced into the dry mountain regions of New Mexico. It is one of several exotic big game species that can now be hunted in the United States.*

Hawaii is exotic. The islands have no native big game species. Aside from wild pigs, feral goats *(Capra hircus)* and feral sheep *(Ovis aries)* are two of the most numerous. They are found on a number of islands. They are reputed to provide very challenging hunting with the big rams and billies being particularly hard to bag.

Hawaii has also imported the mouflon from Europe. This animal is doing well. One idea behind this import was the hope that the mouflon would interbreed with the feral sheep and thereby improve the trophy quality of these sheep. Other imports were the pronghorn antelope and the black-tailed deer from the mainland. Both of these animals are doing well.

There is no doubt that the axis deer *(Axis axis)* is Hawaii's most spectacular big game animal. This attractive, spotted deer bears impressive antlers. It is native to southern Asia, particularly India. The season on axis deer on the island of Lanai is fairly long.

As a biologist, I feel that importing exotic big game species should be viewed with a jaundiced eye. It is always possible that new parasites or diseases can be brought in which might threaten our native big game species or domestic livestock species. A quarantine is not an absolute guarantee that an animal is free of potentially harmful disease organisms or parasites.

An even more important factor to consider is the possible effect of introductions of exotic species on native game. Such impact is difficult to predict with certainty. Some exotic species could become competitors for browse and cover with native species. Also, at times, exotic big game has an aura of panacea. One should remember that there are no shortcuts to game abundance. Nature does not work that way. We could find that a great deal of time and money has been wasted on playing with exotics without any benefit. In the meantime, this money and time could have been used to improve the habitat and increase the carrying capacity of habitats for our native big game species. One of the keys to game abundance is better habitat.

North America has one of the richest varieties of big game mammals in the world. They are part of the ecosystem of this continent. If we manage them along sound ecological principles, they are capable of providing even more hunting and more outdoor recreation, than they have in the past.

Chapter XI

Small Game Mammals

I have always thought of small game mammals as being the bread and butter of hunting. Why? My boyhood memories no doubt have something to do with it. Boys, beagles, and bunnies on sunny wintry days are almost a magic sort of combination that man appreciates a bit more with each year of his life span.

However, the real reason why small game mammals are the basic staple of hunting is because by most standards they are abundant, widely distributed, and are usually good to eat. The lowly cottontail is a good example. It provides more hunting sport than all the ducks and geese combined, and on top of this, it is better to eat than many species of waterfowl.

Perhaps the best thing about small game mammals is that they are a sort of democratic ideal of hunting. Not everyone can afford a trip after woodcock to New Brunswick or an elk hunt in Wyoming, but almost everyone from judges to janitors can go after cottontails or squirrels. Expensive guns, fancy equipment, or lengthy and costly trips are not needed.

THE RABBITS   *Sylvilagus spp.*

The rabbit is probably our most hunted small game mammal. There are three good reasons for this. First, it is very good to eat; second, it is widely distributed; and third, even the farm lands near our major population centers have a surprising abundance of cottontails.

Most hunters don't realize that we have several species of cottontails. The eastern cottontail *(Sylvilagus floridanus)* is the most widely distributed. It ranges from southern Ontario and southern Saskatchewan south to Florida and Mexico. The mountain cottontail *(Sylvilagus nuttalli)* is found in the mountains of the west from northern New Mexico to Washington. The desert cottontail *(Sylvilagus auduboni)* is found in the dry, arid regions from Idaho to Mexico including southern California. The New England cottontail *(Sylvilagus transitionalis)*, as the name suggests, is found predominantly in New England.

All of these cottontail species look very much alike. They are all about the same size, 2 to 3 pounds, with the desert cottontail perhaps being a shade smaller. They all have a tail that looks like a ball of cotton.

There is another group of rabbits also belonging to the genus *Sylvilagus*. The best known of these is the swamp or marsh rabbit *(Sylvilagus palustris)* — the "cane-cutter" of the southern states. Some biologists consider the swamp rabbit of Florida to be a separate species and call it *Sylvilagus aquaticus*, but I doubt if the rabbits recognize the difference.

There is also a brush rabbit *(Sylvilagus bachmani)* in the brush country along the Pacific coast. In the sagebrush country of southern Idaho and in the area where California, Nevada, and Oregon come together, there is the tiny pygmy rabbit *(Sylvilagus idahoensis)*.

The swamp, brush, and pygmy rabbits do not have the white tail of the cottontail. The swamp rabbit is the biggest, weighing 3 to 5 pounds, while the brush rabbit weighs 2 to 2½ pounds, and the pygmy rabbit weighs about one pound.

Hunting Hints — Cottontails thrive wherever there is good brushy cover. The sagebrush plains in the west are good cottontail country. In the east and mid-west, overgrown fence rows, weedy gullies, abandoned fields and orchards, and small brushy woodlots are the places to hunt.

The brown color of the cottontail is its first line of defense. It will crouch down hoping that you will pass by. Hunt slowly, stopping every few steps to look around. This will make the bunny nervous enough to jump out, giving you a shot. Be sure to investigate all thick cover, brush piles, and clumps of tall grass. Kick these out well. This is where bunnies hide.

Rabbit hunting reaches its best form with beagles. These merry little hounds love to trail bunnies. When they get a rabbit running, the bunny always runs in big irregular circles, unwilling to leave its home territory. The idea is for the hunters to figure out where the rabbit will run so that they are in a position to get a shot.

A good cottontail gun is an open choked shotgun from 20 to 12 gauge loaded with No. 6 to 7½ shot. It should be light and fast swinging. A bunny bouncing and dodging along in thick cover is not an easy target. For swamp rabbits, many hunters prefer a bigger shot size — 5's or even 4's.

Another way to hunt rabbits is to stalk them, particularly after a snowfall, as they lie in their forms. This is a technique for the patient, meticulous hunter. It is a good one for archers. You must walk slowly — very slowly — and look carefully. It takes a particular type of experience to be able to spot cottontails crouching in thick cover. Hunters who hunt this way don't look for the whole rabbit, just a part. Most frequently it is the eye that gives the rabbit away. A .22 rifle is the usual weapon for this sport. A bow would certainly add a further dimension.

27. *The cottontail is the bread and butter of hunting. Not everyone can afford to travel after moose or sheep, but everyone can hunt the bunny. Hunting with muzzle loading guns is becoming an increasingly popular sport.*

THE SNOWSHOE HARE   *Lepus americanus*

The snowshoe hare is a mammal of the northern forests where human populations, with a few exceptions, are sparse. The snowshoe is probably our most underharvested game species. It gets its name from its big, furry feet which act as snowshoes. However, a more correct name for the animal is the varying hare, named for the way it varies its color from brown to white depending upon season. In summer, the snowshoe is brown, but as winter approaches its pelt turns to white. The snowshoe hare usually weighs about 3½ pounds.

Hunting Hints — The snowshoe hare is found in the forests from the hills of Virginia and the Great Lakes states through New England across northern Canada into Alaska and south to Colorado and northern California. It is most abundant in young forests growing in logged over areas or in old burns. This is where the animal should be hunted. Hunting techniques are similar to those for cottontails. In some areas, however, the snowshoe is not very wary and will not run away from a hunter. A .22 rifle is a good weapon for such hunting, but a hand gun or a bow is even more sporting.

Hounds add a lot of fun to snowshoe hare hunting, but beagles are usually a little too small for the deep. snow. The bigger hounds are a better choice. Hares run in wider circles than cottontails, and when they are pursued by hounds, they move like white ghosts over the snow, presenting very difficult targets indeed. Since they are generally shot in thick cover at close range, a light, open choked shotgun of 12 to 20 gauge loaded with No. 6 shot is the best bet.

THE JACKRABBITS (HARES)   *Lepus spp.*

The jackrabbits belong to the same order (Lagomorpha) as the rabbits, but they are not rabbits. They are characterized by long ears and long hind legs. The jackrabbits are animals of the open plains and deserts. They are frequently considered agricultural pests and hence classified as varmints which can be hunted at any time. I have included them in this section for three reasons.

First, some states such as Oklahoma, South Dakota, Minnesota, and Wisconsin among others have already given the jackrabbits recognition as game animals with open and closed hunting seasons. Second, since jackrabbits, snowshoe hares, and cottontails are all closely related, it seems logical to include them in the same chapter. Third, although jackrabbits are not usually eaten, they can be really quite good. The secret is in the cooking. Some of the finest meals I have ever eaten were marinated European hare in Germany. The European hare is a highly regarded game species in Europe, both from the standpoint of hunting and on the table. The North American jackrabbits look almost identical to the European hare.

154

There are three species of jackrabbits in North America. The whitetail jackrabbit *(Lepus townsendi)* is a hare of the northern plains. It is found from western Wisconsin and Minnesota west to the foothill country of Oregon and Washington. Its north-south range extends from the prairies of Alberta and Saskatchewan to Colorado.

The whitetail jack is predominantly brown in summer but turns white or pale grey in winter. Its distinguishing features are black tips on the ears and a white tail. It weighs from 6 to 10 pounds.

The blacktail jackrabbit *(Lepus californicus)* is similar in appearance to the whitetail, but the top of the tail is black. The blacktail jack stays brown all year round. It is smaller than the whitetail, running about 4 to 7 pounds.

The blacktail jack is found from the sagebrush plains of Oregon south to Baja California and from Nebraska south to central Mexico. It inhabits the drier, short grass plains and the open deserts.

The antelope jackrabbit *(Lepus alleni)* is found from southeastern New Mexico through the dry plains of northern Mexico and along the Gulf of California. The antelope jack is the biggest of the hares, weighing from 7 to 13 pounds. It has very long ears, without any black on them. The back is brown in color and the sides and belly are whitish. This hare looks like a white flash when it runs through mesquite and other desert vegetation.

The European hare *(Lepus europaeus)* has been stocked in several areas of eastern North America. It is still occasionally found in the open farm lands of New York, New Jersey, Connecticut, and Massachusetts, and is quite abundant in areas of southern Ontario.

In appearance the European hare looks like the blacktail jackrabbit or the whitetail in its summer peltage. The tail of the European hare is black on top and whitish on the sides. The animal weighs 7 to 12 pounds.

The Arctic hare *(Lepus arcticus)* is a large hare of 6 to 12 pounds. On many of the islands in the high Arctic, it remains white throughout the year, but on the mainland of Labrador through the tundra of the Northwest Territories and Alaska, it turns brown with the coming of spring. In the older biology texts, the Arctic hare of Alaska is called the tundra hare *(Lepus othus)*, but I doubt that the hares recognize any difference between themselves, regardless of what the old school biologists claim.

Hunting Hints — When jacks are numerous, drives are sometimes organized by hunters and ranchers to reduce their numbers. A group of hunters simply walk in line about a hundred yards apart over the prairie. A good safe choice for this type of hunting is a full choked shotgun loaded with No. 4 shot.

A couple of hunters can jump jacks by walking slowly through areas where the hares lie up during the day. The sportiest gun for this type of hunting is a light varmint rifle with a moderate scope. A running hare is not an easy target. They have been clocked running at over 40 miles per hour. A rifleman who can consistently hit running jacks will find deer and antelope easy.

The thing to remember is that jacks are most active in the morning and evening. This is a very good time to hunt them because they can frequently be seen hopping about in the open.

Jacks can also be hunted with coursing hounds such as greyhounds or whippets. These are about the only two breeds of dogs, except perhaps for a hunting saluki or Afghan hound, that can on occasion run down a hare. A few individuals still practice this old and exciting sport in the west.

In Ontario, European hares are also hunted by drives, but usually with only 5 or 6 hunters. Some hunters also use hounds such as foxhounds, black and tans, blueticks, and very large beagles to hunt the hares. The basic method is the same as fox hunting, with the hares being shot in front of the hounds. Full choked 12 gauge shotguns with No. 4 or No. 2 shot are generally used.

THE SQUIRRELS $\qquad$ *Sciurus* spp.

The squirrels rank next to rabbits as our most popular small game mammal. Indeed, in many areas, particularly the south, there are more squirrel hunters than rabbit hunters. There is no doubt that squirrels are harder to bag than cottontails. They are harder to outwit.

There are several species of tree squirrels in North America, but only the gray and the fox are considered game. The little red squirrel *(Tamiasciurus hudsonicus)* is not hunted.

The eastern gray squirrel *(Sciurus carolinensis)* is found from southern Ontario to eastern Texas and from Maine to North Dakota. The western gray squirrel *(Sciurus griseus)* is found in the Pacific states from California to Washington. There is also an Arizona gray squirrel *(Sciurus arizonensis)* which is found in Arizona and northern Mexico.

All three species of gray squirrels are very similar in appearance. They weigh from 1 to 1½ pounds. The western gray has a slightly bluish tinge. The eastern gray is not always grey in color. There is also a black color phase. In some parts of Canada, the black phase is more common than the gray.

The fox squirrel *(Sciurus niger)* is another important game species. It is found from Pennsylvania to Iowa and from North Dakota to Texas. The fox squirrel is larger than the gray. Exceptional specimens can weigh up to 3 pounds, but 2 to 2½ pounds are more common. The fox squirrel gets its name from the color of its coat; it is rusty and yellowish, similar to a red fox. Again there are different color phases ranging from grey to black.

The tassel-eared squirrel *(Sciurus alberti)* is the least known of the squirrels. This is not surprising because it is found only in the pine forests of Arizona. The tassel-eared squirrel is an attractive animal with grey sides, and a reddish back with a whitish or black belly. The tail is whitish on the underside. The key characteristic of this species is the dark colored tassels or tufts on the ears. The tassel-eared squirrel is approximately the size of the eastern gray.

Hunting Hints — One of the finest ways to hunt squirrels is by taking a stand in good squirrel woods at dawn. As soon as the sun rises, the squirrels come out of their dens to feed. The hunter must be perfectly still and have sharp eyes. This is a rifleman's sport. The best weapon is an accurate .22 rifle with a scope sight. The hunter must be a good shot because the ranges vary from 30 to 80 yards.

Walking very slowly through squirrel woods and watching sharply is another good hunting technique. A hunting partner is a real asset because squirrels dodge around the tree as the hunter circles. But a squirrel can't escape by dodging around a tree when there are two hunters. A shotgun, tight choked with No. 6 shot, is the best gun for this type of hunting because the squirrels are usually running or leaping from tree to tree.

Another way to hunt squirrels is with dogs. Squirrel dogs are generally small mixed breeds with a predominance of terrier blood. The dogs search through the woods using both their eyes and nose, and when they have a squirrel treed, they bark to attract the hunter. This hunting method is probably not as popular as it used to be, but in the hill country of the south, feisty little squirrel dogs are still quite common.

Squirrel hunters should always be constantly on the watch for squirrel signs such as fragments and cuttings of nuts and acorns. This is a good clue that squirrels are around. Indeed, on a still morning, a hunter on a stand can frequently hear cuttings drop to the leaves. Many a squirrel has been bagged because the hunter used his ears. Trained eyes are also very important in bushytail hunting. An experienced hunter always sees more squirrels than a tyro. The beginners look for the entire squirrel, while the experts look only for an ear sticking out, the tip of a tail, or even an unusual bump on a limb that may be a squirrel lying flat.

The best time to hunt squirrels is in the early morning or late afternoon. The bushytails are more active then. Calm, warm, windless days are best. When it is cold and windy, the bushytails are in their holes or nests sleeping. Another good time is after a rain, particularly if the sun has come out. The squirrels will come out to feed. In the warm days of the early season, don't expect much activity at mid-day. That is siesta time for bushytails. A wise hunter takes a clue from the squirrels.

THE RACCOON
Procyon lotor

The raccoon, generally considered a game animal because it is hunted mainly for sport, is also classified as a fur bearing animal because of its fine fur. In recent years, raccoon pelts have been bringing in quite high prices.

In some states and provinces, however, the raccoon is classified as a varmint and is given no protection. This generally occurs in states with large 'coon populations and very few 'coon hunters.

Raccoons have a wide range. They can be found from the bleak shores of Hudson Bay south to Key West and from northern Alberta south to Mexico. They are found from coast to coast and indeed many of the coastal marshes have high populations of raccoons.

Hunting Hints — 'Coon hunting is a great American tradition. Some hunters may not equate it with as fine a sport as quail shooting or duck hunting, but there is no doubt that the roots of raccoon hunting go as deeply as the roots of either quail or duck hunting. There is only one way to look at it — each hunter to his own. But I can chase 'coons half the night, be up huddling in a duck blind well before dawn, and when the sun has risen well over the horizon, follow my bird dogs until dusk.

I have found that people who look down on 'coon hunting frequently also look down on cottontail hunting. In most cases it's because they have never tried it and unfortunately sometimes it is a sort of class prejudice suffered by stuffed-shirt snobs. 'Coon hunting is largely a sport of the farmers, the hill country folk, the mechanics, but this does not mean that it is not exciting or a lot of fun. Some of my fondest memories come from boyhood 'coon hunts.

When a raccoon is in danger, it climbs into a tree. This is the weak link in 'coon behaviour on which raccoon hunting methods were developed. All you have to do is chase a 'coon up a tree and you've got him. At least that's the theory. The problem is getting the 'coon up the right tree.

Raccoon hunting is responsible for the development of several breeds of hounds bred especially for the sport. The best known breeds are the black and tan, the bluetick, the redbone, and the treeing Walker. The hounds are taken into areas where 'coons are abundant and released. When they find a 'coon track, the hounds trail the animal, baying on the trail. When the hounds get close, the 'coon climbs up a tree to get away. The hounds stay at the bottom of the tree and call "treed" with excited baying. The hunters then walk to the tree and either take the hounds away to look for another 'coon or if they want the pelt, they shoot the coon usually with a .22 rifle. To tree a raccoon, even with a well trained hound, is not easy. The 'coons have numerous methods of losing hounds — by swimming, climbing from tree to tree, running on the top of rail fences, and hiding in hollow den trees.

It is difficult to pick the best state for 'coon hunting. Southern Ontario may be one of the best; certainly 'coon hunting is Ontario is not particularly popular and 'coons are so abundant that they are considered a varmint.

158

THE OPOSSUM

Didelphis marsupialis

The opossum is a primitive mammal belonging to the order Marsupialia, the pouch bearing mammals. The young are incubated in the pouch. Kangaroos are perhaps the best known members of the marsupial order.

The opossum is approximately the size of a house cat. It has a long pointed snout, and short erect ears which are hairless. It has a long hairless tail which the animal can use to wrap around a branch and hang. Its feet strongly resemble those of a monkey. The opossum is a good tree climber.

The opossum's range extends from southern New Hampshire and southern Ontario to Florida and Mexico, and from coast to coast.

Hunting Hints — Opossums are hunted with hounds just like raccoons. However, the opossum has neither the speed nor the intelligence of the raccoon. When a hound gets on an opossum trail, the chase is generally short and the opossum is treed. A treed opossum is usually shot down with a .22 rifle.

Any sort of hound can be used for opossums. Discarded 'coon hounds, the ones who could not cut the mustard on raccoon hunts, are frequently used for opossums. Opossum hunting doesn't have quite the excitement of 'coon hunting, mainly because the quarry is much easier to bag. Yet the hound music is the same and certainly scrambling through the woods and swamps is just as difficult. One other tip I can offer is that hunting is best on moonless nights. Opossums seem to roam about more on dark, cloudy nights.

Opossum hunting is mainly practiced in the south where opossum meat and sweet potatoes are relished by many people. The fur also has a small commercial value.

Chapter XII

Varmints

The usual definition of a varmint (derived from the word vermin) is a species of wildlife that causes damage to man's interests. A bounty has frequently been paid to kill varmints. Sometimes varmints have done agricultural damage, but more often they were predators on game to which man felt he had first claim.

Far worse than the bounty payments were the mass poisoning campaigns waged by our governments on coyotes and prairie dogs. Along with these two species, the poisoning campaigns were responsible for the destruction of such creatures as the kit fox and the black-footed ferret. The government "predator hunters" who performed this task were frequently so zealous in their duties that they carried out their macabre work even where the coyotes and prairie dogs were causing no damage.

There is no doubt that animals such as woodchucks can be farm pests or that occasionally coyotes kill lambs on sheep ranches in the west. When this happens, the offending animals should be removed — killed. However, in our enlightened age, we should not tolerate the payment of bounties for the wholesale condemnation of some of the more interesting creatures of the animal kingdom.

The term varmint is very fluid. I know farmers who view the fox as nothing but a nuisance animal, and I know hunters, still riding to hounds, to whom a fox tail — the brush — is a highly regarded trophy. In short, what is a varmint in one area can be a highly valued game animal in another. Some states give protection to foxes and woodchucks while others do not. I firmly believe that many so-called varmints should be given protection at least during the times when their young are being raised. And sometime in the not-too-distant future, I am certain they will be.

I also feel that bounties should be abolished. They stem from a time when we tried to solve our wildlife management problems with traps, poison, and guns. Wildlife management is the science of applied ecology and ecological solutions are not that simple. Besides, we are finding that frequently the damage caused by foxes, coyotes, and crows is more imaginary than real. One thing few hunters will argue about is that many of the so-called varmints are more challenging and more exciting to hunt than the game species, as anyone who has hunted cottontails and foxes well knows.

THE 'CHUCKS   *Marmota* spp.

The woodchuck *(Marmota monax)* is a well known creature of the eastern farm lands. It is generally considered to be an agricultural pest, but some states give it protection during the early summer. The woodchuck has two western cousins — the rockchuck, more properly called the yellow-bellied marmot *(Marmota flaviventris)* and the hoary marmot *(Marmota caligata)* of the high mountains.

The woodchuck's range extends from Labrador south to Louisiana and north through the mid-west to central Alaska. The rockchuck is found from the lower slopes of British Columbia through Idaho to California and Colorado. The hoary marmot extends through the high alpine meadows and talus slopes of the high mountains from northern Alaska and the Yukon to Washington and Idaho.

All of the marmots have similar life histories. Even in appearance, they resemble one another very closely. Because the woodchuck is by far the most important of the three to the hunter, I will describe its life history much more closely. The woodchuck is one animal that has benefited from the felling of forests. Although woodchucks do live in forests, they are much more abundant in farm country. Farm 'chucks grow larger than those of the forest; they can weigh up to 10 pounds.

The woodchuck, or groundhog as it is commonly called, is a burrowing animal that excavates dens for itself. Dens, with their mounds of earth at the entrance, are a hazard to farm machinery and livestock. Woodchucks are strictly vegetarian and do not hesitate to raid gardens, but usually feed in hay fields and pastures. For these reasons, the woodchuck has not endeared itself to farmers who frequently welcome hunters after 'chucks.

Hunting Hints — Woodchucks prefer rolling or hilly farm country where light soils are easy to dig. This is where they are the most abundant, and this is where the hunter should concentrate his effort. 'Chucks are most active in the morning and evening, resting in their burrows during the heat of mid-day. Hence morning and evening is the time to hunt them. Good binoculars are an asset for a woodchuck hunt.

Many rifles and telescopic sights are made primarily for sniping woodchuck at long ranges. The woodchuck rifle needs to be very accurate because the 'chuck at 250 or 300 yards is a small target. In thickly settled farm country, a .222 calibre is probably the best. It does not make too much noise. But more powerful cartridges can be used in less populated areas.

Woodchucks can also be hunted by stalking them to within range with a .22 rimfire, a bow, or a handgun.

Neither the hoary marmot nor the rockchuck are hunted as much as the woodchuck. However, the rockchuck can be something of a pest on some western ranches and is hunted by riflemen. Any rifle suitable for woodchucks should be fine for these two marmots. However, since both these animals live in remote, unpopulated areas, more powerful rifles can be used because rifle fire noise is not an important factor.

Young woodchucks make fine eating, particularly when the excess fat is trimmed away. They are parboiled lightly, and then barbecued.

THE PRAIRIE DOGS
Cynomys spp.

The prairie dogs are not, of course, even remotely related to dogs. They are rodents, but because they issue a shrill, yapping, bark-like sound when alarmed, they were given the name prairie dogs.

There are two species of prairie dogs — the blacktail prairie dog *(Cynomys ludovicianus)* and the whitetail prairie dog *(Cynomys gunnisoni)*. There are also two subspecies of the whitetail prairie dog which are considered to be separate species by some biologists.

The blacktail prairie dog is distributed from southern Alberta and Saskatchewan southward through the great plains right to Mexico. The whitetail prairie dog has a smaller distribution, extending from the valleys of southern Montana through the foothills of the western mountains southward to central Arizona and New Mexico.

Adult prairie dogs look very similar to ground squirrels. The prairie dog is about 15 inches long and weighs 1½ to 3 pounds. It is, at times, mistaken for a ground squirrel, or more commonly, ground squirrels are mistaken for prairie dogs. Prairie dogs always live in colonies called "towns".

Hunting Hints — Prairie dogs may be in danger of extinction. Certainly their numbers have been reduced drastically by government-employed poisoners and by ranchers. The greatest sin of prairie dogs is that they eat grass, and grass is needed for cattle. But in many cases, prairie dogs lived on marginal grazing lands which were not used by cattle. They were poisoned anyway, with gas or poisoned grain. Prairie dogs were sometimes accused of overgrazing the grasslands because they were most abundant on overgrazed lands. In actuality, ecologists have shown that prairie dogs were the symptoms of poor agricultural practices on the part of ranchers, not the cause.

Today prairie dogs survive in a few national parks and ranches with tiny bits of marginal land. Some of these ranches keep the prairie dogs around for nostalgic reasons, as a reminder of the old west. Other ranchers would have poisoned them out long ago, had not the odd varmint hunter from town kept the prairie dog population down with his "fancy" varmint rifle.

163

It seems almost immoral to give instructions as to how to hunt prairie dogs, but I will. Why? For two reasons. Had prairie dogs been a game animal, they would have been reasonably abundant today, like cottontails. We hunters would have seen to it. The second reason is that a few prairie dog towns survive on western ranches because they are hunted by the rancher's friends. If the hunters had not kept the prairie dogs under control, the rancher would have — with poison — and there is no way to limit poisoning.

Prairie dogs are most active in the cool of the morning and late afternoon. This is the time to hunt them. During the heat of midday, prairie dogs are in their burrows taking a siesta.

The hunter should approach the prairie dog town within rifle range and conceal himself. At his approach, the prairie dogs will scurry into their holes. Once the hunter has concealed himself, they will begin to emerge. Although the crack of the rifle will alarm them, they will not stay below ground for long if the rifleman remains hidden.

It sometimes is possible to stalk the prairie dog like a woodchuck, but not often. The prairie dog town is generally located on flat, barren land with little cover to conceal the stalking hunter. There may be places where a hunter can get close enough to prairie dogs to hunt them with a .22 rimfire, but generally a cartridge with a longer range will have to be used. Since noise is generally not a factor in the unsettled west, such cartridges as the .22-250, the .243, 6 mm, and .25,06 are good choices. A 'scope sight is a must. Anything from 8 to 12 power would be a good bet. The rifle has to be very accurate. Prairie dogs are small targets.

Prairie dogs can be eaten, but most people don't care for the "earthy" taste. Indians ate prairie dogs whenever they could kill them easily.

I strongly believe that more drastic conservation action is needed to insure that prairie dogs will survive. Perhaps the way to start is for state and federal governments to purchase lands — sort of mini-state or national parks — with prairie dog colonies. In this way, the colony would be protected from potential harm. The purchase of such land would be an excellent project for sportsmen's clubs. A damn fine way to show the non-hunting public that sportsmen are interested in conserving wildlife species other than game species.

Another possibility might be to start new colonies on state or national parks by live-trapping and transplanting prairie dogs. I don't know the ecological feasibility of such a plan, but it certainly should be investigated, if it has not already been done.

By saving the prairie dog, we also save the black-footed ferret, the prairie dog's arch predator. This large weasel lives solely on prairie dogs. When the prairie dog populations were decimated, the black-footed ferret died along with them. Today, this ferret is in grave danger of extinction, much more so than the prairie dog.

I hope that prairie dogs will bark and whistle in alarm for many generations to come and that black-footed ferrets will stalk them for the same time. They are a part of the old west, of the virgin plains. If prairie dogs were to disappear, we would lose an important part of our heritage.

THE FOXES
Vulpes spp. and others

There are generally considered to be four species of foxes in North America. Both the red fox and the gray fox are well known, while the Arctic fox and the kit fox are lesser known.

The Arctic fox *(Alopex lagopus)* is an attractive white or light blue-grey fox living in the Arctic tundra. Because of its valuable fur, the animal is trapped by Eskimos, but never hunted for sport.

The kit fox *(Vulpes macrotis)* is a small prairie fox weighing a mere 4 to 5 pounds. It has large ears and its pelt is buffy grey in color. The kit fox is a swift runner and occasionally is called the swift fox. At one time the swift fox *(Vulpes velox)* was thought to be a different species, but biologists now generally regard the kit fox and the swift fox as the same animal. The kit fox is quite rare and is perhaps in danger. It was a victim of the mass poisoning campaigns against coyotes. It is not hunted.

The gray fox *(Urocyon cinereoargenteus)* is fairly abundant across most of the southern and eastern United States, including Mexico, and has recently extended its range into southern Ontario, Quebec, and Manitoba. The gray fox runs about 8 to 12 pounds and prefers wooded country rather than open farm land. This fox is well known for its tree climbing ability.

The best known of all the foxes is the red fox *(Vulpes vulpes)*, the most widely distributed fox in North America. The range of this fox extends from the Bering Strait to the coast of Newfoundland and south to southern California and Louisiana. The sly reynard, well known for its elusiveness and intelligence, is about the same size as the gray fox. It is not always red in color as the name might indicate. Several well known color phases occur in the north such as black, and the silver phase of the fur trade.

Hunting Hints — There are several methods of hunting foxes, the most exciting being with hounds. There are two types of hound chases. In the formal fox hunt, the hunters, dressed in scarlet livery, ride to hounds. Although there are hunt clubs still in existence, they seldom chase foxes because of fences and crop lands.

The other type of fox chase is with 2 or 3 hounds. The hunters set out in the early morning, preferably after a fresh snowfall, to look for fresh tracks. The hounds are released on fresh tracks and the hunters try to intercept the fox to get a shot at it. Foxes run in irregular circles within their own territory, and getting a shot at a fox is not too easy. The fox is too intelligent and has too sharp a nose and eyesight to be easily bagged. A full-choked 12 gauge shotgun loaded with No. 4 or 2 shot is the best weapon for a fox chase.

There are other methods of hunting foxes that are totally different. One method is to walk through good fox country in the winter with a rifle, tracking the animals and hoping to get a shot. An even better way is to glass the sunny, snow covered hillsides for foxes sleeping in the warm sun. The hunter then stalks the fox within rifle range.

Hunting foxes with a predator call has also become a popular method. The call sounds like the squeals of an injured rabbit. The fox slinks to the sound hoping for an easy meal, and possibly offering the hunter a shot. Outwitting a fox with a rabbit call is not easy. There are a variety of predator calls on the market, including phonograph records with calling instructions and hunting tips. The best time to call foxes is at dawn or dusk. This is a sport for the patient hunter who enjoys outwitting one of nature's slyest creatures.

The fox has been considered a varmint, frequently with a price on its head, for many years. Slowly we are learning that the fox is not the villain we thought it to be, and bounties are being abolished. Some day we may even be wise enough to declare the fox a small game mammal everywhere. Certainly a fox is much harder to bag than most commonly hunted game mammals.

THE COYOTE *Canis latrans*

The wail of a coyote, the howl of a timberwolf, and the honking of geese are nostalgic sounds to every outdoorsman. They epitomize wild things and wilderness. Without the coyote's wild wail, the western plains and foothills would not be the same.

The coyote is a small grey wolf with a drooping bushy tail. On the prairies the coyote weighs about 25 pounds and is sometimes referred to as the prairie wolf. In the hardwood or mixed forest of the east, it is known as the brush wolf and can weigh nearly twice as much as the prairie coyote.

Hunting Hints — The coyote can be hunted basically by the same techniques used for the fox. Large hounds can be used to chase the coyote, while hunters try to intercept it. Although this is not widely practiced, some hunters in the Great Lakes area have hounds trained for this. A full-choked 12 gauge shotgun loaded with No. 2 shot or BB's is the best weapon for such coyote hunts, but some hunters prefer rifles.

In the west, a rifleman can walk out onto the prairie and hunt coyotes by glassing for them at dawn and dusk. The hunter attempts to stalk a coyote once he has spotted one. A flat shooting, accurate rifle of at least .243 caliber with a scope sight is needed for this type of hunting.

Probably the best way to hunt coyotes, and certainly one of the more popular ways of hunting them in the southwestern United States, is with

166

predator calls. Coyotes are generally more susceptible to calling than foxes.

The coyote is one animal that has learned to take care of itself and multiply against insurmountable odds. However opinions of men are changing and we are looking at the coyote in a new and wiser light. Bounties are being abandoned. The coyote is intelligent and difficult to hunt. It is more than a match for any hunter.

THE BOBCAT   *Lynx ruffus*

Because of its shy and retiring nature, the bobcat is rarely seen, even by those who spend much time outdoors. The bobcat closely resembles the lynx *(Lynx canadensis)*, although its fur is of no great commercial value. The lynx, a very valuable fur bearing animal, is never hunted for sport, although a few states do classify it as a varmint.

The bobcat is characterized by short ear tufts and a black spot on the tail, while the lynx has long, black ear tufts and a completely black-tipped tail. Bobcat toms weigh on the average about 25 pounds, while the females are about 10 pounds lighter.

Hunting Hints — The bobcat is hunted in much the same way as the cougar. Hounds follow it and "tree" it or bring it to bay under fallen trees or crevices among rocks. Hunters take their hounds into bobcat country and let the dogs search for a fresh trail. In winter, hunters may drive along logging roads looking for fresh tracks. The hounds are then released on the fresh tracks. Certainly a bobcat hunt with hounds is a thrilling experience. More often than not the bobcat gives the hounds the slip. Most hunters today do not shoot the cat, but prefer to take the hounds away to let the cat live for many more chases. A bobcat skin does, however, make an interesting trophy.

Bobcats can also be hunted with a predator call like foxes and coyotes. Bobcats generally come to the call very stealthily. Many times a hunter doesn't even know that the bobcat has stalked close to him and left. It is not easy to get a shot at a bobcat by calling. In fact, most bobcats taken in this way are called in incidentally by fox and coyote hunters.

Bobcats are found through most of southern Canada and the United States, with exception to some of the heavily populated areas of the midwest and central states. They are, however, found in the wooded areas of the Mississippi River valley.

THE CROWS   *Corvus* spp.

One group of birds that has certainly benefited from modern agriculture has been the crows. There are probably more crows now than there were 300 years ago and although this animal is something of a villain, it should probably not be painted as black as it sometimes is.

The eastern crow *(Corvus brachyrhynchos)*, or common crow as it is sometimes called, is distributed over most of North America except Mexico. The fish crow *(Corvus ossifragus)* is common along the Atlantic and gulf coasts. As its name indicates, this crow is known to eat fish, but like the rest of the crows, it is almost completely omnivorous. The northwestern crow *(Corvus caurinus)* is found along the northwest coast of the Alaskan mainland south to the state of Washington.

Hunting Hints — Crows are most active in the early morning and this is the best time to hunt them. Activity picks up again later in the afternoon. Early mornings, however, are best. One way to hunt crows is by pass shooting on a flyway leading to and from a roosting site. This is particularly effective in prairie country where shooting sites are at a premium. Hunters simply hide on the route which the crows use and when the birds come into range, they start shooting. Shooting right at the roost is also good, but this will cause the birds to abandon the roost. If you are out to destroy as many crows as possible, shoot at the roost. If you want continuous shooting, shoot the flyway.

The best and most exciting way to hunt crows is over a great horned owl. The great horn is the traditional enemy of crows and vice versa. Crows will attack an owl whenever they find one. Most hunters use plastic or papier mâché owl decoys, but a live owl is by far the best. A few enthusiastic crow hunters keep owls for that purpose. A decoy owl backed with the war cry of the crow either from a crow call in the mouth of a hunter or from an electronic caller will really bring the black bandits in. Be sure to have a good blind and keep out of sight. Once crows see a human, they know they have been fooled and the game is over. A good gun for this type of shooting is one with a fairly open choke and loaded with No. 7½ shot.

Crows are abundant in most of the farming areas of Canada and the United States, and are not generally protected by any game laws. The crow does not need protection. It is one bird that can take care of itself.

OTHER VARMINTS

There are several other species of birds and mammals generally classified as varmints. However, none is hunted to any great extent.

Various species of ground squirrels *(Citellus* spp.*)* are considered varmints. They are frequently but erroneously lumped together and called "gophers" The Franklin ground squirrel is perhaps the most common, but others are the Richardson's ground squirrel, the 13-lined ground squirrel frequently called the "striped gopher", and several others. They are all fairly small and generally not hunted except by farm boys with .22 rifles. These "gophers" can be something of a nuisance in ranching and farming country.

The armadillo found through Texas, Oklahoma, Louisiana, and Florida is generally not protected. The badger is another animal that is frequently not protected. However, I feel it should be, because it preys primarily on rodents.

In some states porcupines are not protected because of the damage they do to trees, while in other states such small predators as weasels, skunks, and civet cats are on the predator list. Even the lynx is not protected everywhere as a fur bearing animal. None of these animals are hunted intentionally.

Several species of small birds such as starlings, red-winged blackbirds, cowbirds, and English sparrows are regarded as agricultural pests and receive no protection. The magpie of the western states and provinces is usually classified as a varmint. This long-tailed black and white bird occasionally preys on bird nests, eating both eggs and young. However, it is not a serious pest and usually not as numerous as its cousin the crow. It is not hunted very much nor is it easy to hunt. Its flight is tricky, providing challenging shotgunning. The bird itself is not a large target for the rifleman. The magpie is as intelligent as the crow.

Certainly today no bird of prey should ever be shot. Indeed, most are protected by law. We now know that none of the owls, hawks, and eagles do as much damage to game birds and domestic stock as formerly believed. Indeed, most are wholly beneficial in their destruction of small rodents. Many of the hawk species are fighting for survival against DDT and other pesticides. In fact, some birds such as the peregrine falcon are very likely already extinct in eastern North America.

I have always had a great deal of admiration for the birds of prey. The life of many hawks and owls is totally committed to hunting. My admiration must stem at least partially from envy. To see a prairie falcon "stoop" — dive — after a bird is a sight that no outdoorsman can ever forget. It is the very essence of hunting. In another age, another time, I would have been an enthusiastic falconer.

Chapter XIII

Where to Hunt

The major game species of every state and province are listed in this chapter. The letter "G" appearing behind the game indicates that the state's fish and game officials consider hunting for that species to be exceptionally good in proper habitats. The address of all game departments is also given so that you can write to them for seasons, regulations, licence costs, guide lists, lists of public hunting areas or public lands open to hunting, and other hunting information.

UNITED STATES

Alabama

Department of Conservation and Natural Resources
64 North Union Street
Montgomery, Alabama 36104

whitetail deer (G), bobwhite quail, turkeys, doves (G), woodcock, snipe, rails, ducks, geese, rabbits (G), squirrels

Alaska

Department of Fish and Game
Subport Building
Juneau, Alaska 99801

moose (G), caribou (G), blacktail deer, elk, Dall sheep, mountain goats, bison, musk oxen, black bear (G), grizzly bear (G), brown bear, wolves, ptarmigan (G), ruffed grouse, spruce grouse, blue grouse, sharptail grouse, snipe, ducks (G), geese (G), snowshoe hares (G)

Arizona

Arizona Game and Fish Department
2222 West Greenway Road
Phoenix, Arizona 85023

whitetail deer, mule deer, pronghorn antelope, elk, desert bighorn sheep, javelina, black bear, cougar, Gambel's quail (G), Mearn's quail (G), scaled quail, ringneck pheasants, wild turkeys, doves (G), ducks

Arkansas
Hunting Information
Arkansas Game and Fish Commission
Little Rock, Arkansas 72201

whitetail deer (G), bobwhite quail, wild turkeys, doves (G), ducks, geese, fox and gray squirrels (G), cottontail rabbits (G)

California
Conservation Program Officer
California Department of Fish and Game
1416 Ninth Street
Sacramento, California 95814

whitetail deer, blacktail deer, elk, pronghorn antelope, wild pigs, black bear, cougar, California quail (G), Gambel's quail, mountain quail, ruffed grouse, blue grouse, sage grouse, wild turkeys, ringneck pheasants, chukar (G), doves (G), bandtail pigeons, ducks (G), geese, gray squirrels, cottontail rabbits (G), jackrabbits

Colorado
Information and Education Office
Colorado Game, Fish and Parks Division
6060 Broadway
Denver, Colorado 80216

mule deer, whitetail deer, elk, pronghorn antelope, bighorn sheep, black bear, cougar, Gambel's quail, scaled quail, bobwhite quail, sharptail grouse, sage grouse, blue grouse, ptarmigan, wild turkeys, chukar, ringneck pheasants, cottontail rabbits (G), jackrabbits, snowshoe hares

Connecticut
Wildlife Unit
Connecticut Department of Environmental Protection
State Office Building
Hartford, Connecticut 06109

whitetail deer, black bear, ringneck pheasants, ruffed grouse, bobwhite quail, woodcock, ducks, geese, cottontail rabbits, snowshoe hares, gray squirrels (G)

Delaware
Delaware Board of Game and Fish Commissioners
Dover, Delaware 19901
> whitetail deer, ringneck pheasants, bobwhite quail (G), woodcock, doves, rails (G), ducks (G), geese (G), cottontail rabbits, gray squirrels

Florida
Information and Education Director
Florida Game and Fresh Water Fish Commission
Bryant Building
Tallahassee, Florida 32304
> whitetail deer (G), black bear, wild pigs, bobwhite quail (G), wild turkeys (G), doves (G), woodcock, snipe, ducks (G), geese, cottontail rabbits (G), marsh rabbits, gray squirrels (G), fox squirrels

Georgia
Public Relations and Information Department
Georgia Department of Natural Resources
270 Washington Street
Atlanta, Georgia 30334
> whitetail deer, black bear, bobwhite quail (G), ruffed grouse, wild turkeys, woodcock, doves (G), ducks, geese, cottontail rabbits (G), gray and fox squirrels (G)

Hawaii
Division of Fish and Game
530 S. Hotel Street
Honolulu, Hawaii 96813
> blacktail deer, axis deer, wild pigs (G), feral sheep (G), mouflon, feral goats (G), pronghorn antelope, wild turkeys, ringneck pheasants, Japanese quail, California quail, Gambel's quail, chukar, gray francolin, black francolin, barred, lace-necked and mourning doves (G)

Idaho
Idaho Department of Fish and Game
600 South Walnut Street
Boise, Idaho 83707
> whitetail deer, mule deer (G), pronghorn antelope (G), elk (G), black bear, bighorn sheep, mountain goats, moose, ringneck pheasants, ruffed grouse, blue grouse (G), sharptail grouse, sage grouse, California quail, bobwhite quail, mountain quail, Hungarian partridge (G), chukar, wild turkeys, ducks (G), geese, cottontail rabbits (G), jackrabbits (G), snowshoe hares

Illinois

Illinois Department of Conservation
102 State Office Building
Springfield, Illinois 62706

> whitetail deer, ringneck pheasants, Hungarian partridges, bobwhite quail (G), wild turkeys, doves (G), ducks, geese (G), cottontail rabbits (G), gray and fox squirrels (G)

Indiana

Indiana Division of Fish and Wildlife
607 State Office Building
Indianapolis, Indiana 46204

> whitetail deer, ringneck pheasants, Hungarian partridges, bobwhite quail, ruffed grouse, woodcock, ducks, geese, cottontail rabbits (G), gray and fox squirrels (G)

Iowa

Information and Education Department
Iowa State Conservation Commission
300 Fourth Street
Des Moines, Iowa 50319

> whitetail deer, ringneck pheasants (G), Hungarian partridges, bobwhite quail (G), ruffed grouse, ducks, geese, cottontail rabbits (G), gray and fox squirrels (G)

Kansas

Kansas Forestry, Fish and Game Commission
Box 1028
Pratt, Kansas 67124

> whitetail deer, mule deer, ringneck pheasants (G), prairie chickens, scaled quail, bobwhite quail (G), doves (G), ducks (G), geese, snipe, cottontail rabbits (G), jackrabbits, gray and fox squirrels

Kentucky

Kentucky Department of Fish and Wildlife Resources
State Office Building Annex
Frankfort, Kentucky 40601

> whitetail deer, bobwhite quail, ruffed grouse, wild turkeys, doves (G), woodcock, ducks, geese, cottontail rabbits, gray squirrels (G), fox squirrels

174

Louisiana

Louisiana Wildlife and Fisheries Commission
400 Royal Street
New Orleans, Louisiana 70130

> whitetail deer (G), bobwhite quail (G), wild turkeys, doves (G), woodcock (G), snipe, rails, ducks (G), geese (G), cottontail rabbits (G), marsh rabbits, gray and fox squirrels

Maine

Maine Department of Inland Fisheries and Game
State House
Augusta, Maine 04330

> whitetail deer (G), black bear (G), ruffed grouse (G), spruce grouse, ringneck pheasants, woodcock (G), ducks (G), geese, gray squirrels, cottontail rabbits, snowshoe hares (G)

Maryland

Maryland Fish and Wildlife Administration
State Office Building
Annapolis, Maryland 21401

> whitetail deer, ringneck pheasants, bobwhite quail (G), wild turkeys, ruffed grouse, woodcock (G), snipe (G), rails (G), doves, ducks (G), geese (G), gray and fox squirrels, cottontail rabbits (G), snowshoe hares

Massachusetts

Information and Education Section
Massachusetts Fish and Game Division
Westboro, Massachusetts 01581

> whitetail deer, black bear, ringneck pheasants, bobwhite quail, ruffed grouse (G), woodcock, rails, ducks, geese, gray squirrels (G), cottontail rabbits, snowshoe hares

Michigan

Michigan Department of Natural Resources
Mason Building
Lansing, Michigan 48926

> whitetail deer, black bear, ringneck pheasants, bobwhite quail, ruffed grouse (G), woodcock (G), ducks, geese, gray and fox squirrels, cottontail rabbits, snowshoe hares (G)

Minnesota
Minnesota Game and Fish Division
390 Centennial Building
St. Paul, Minnesota 55101

> whitetail deer, moose, black bear, ringneck pheasants, Hungarian partridges, ruffed grouse (G), sharptail grouse, woodcock (G), ducks, geese, gray and fox squirrels, cottontail rabbits, snowshoe hares (G)

Mississippi
Mississippi Game and Fish Commission
Box 451
Jackson, Mississippi 39205

> whitetail deer (G), bobwhite quail (G), wild turkeys (G), doves (G), woodcock, ducks (G), geese, gray squirrels (G), fox squirrels, cottontail rabbits (G), swamp rabbits

Missouri
Missouri Department of Conservation
Jefferson City, Missouri 65101

> whitetail deer, ringneck pheasants, bobwhite quail, wild turkeys, doves (G), ducks, geese, cottontail rabbits, jackrabbits, fox and gray squirrels (G)

Montana
Montana Fish and Game Department
Helena, Montana 59601

> whitetail deer, mule deer (G), elk (G), moose, pronghorn antelope (G) bighorn sheep, mountain goats, grizzly bear, black bear (G), cougar, ringneck pheasants, Hungarian partridges (G), chukar, ruffed grouse, sharptail grouse, sage grouse, wild turkeys, ducks (G), geese, cottontail rabbits, jack rabbits, snowshoe hares

Nebraska
Nebraska Game Commission
State Capitol Building
Lincoln, Nebraska 68509

> whitetail deer, mule deer, pronghorn antelope, ringneck pheasants (G), bobwhite quail (G), sharptail grouse, prairie chickens, wild turkeys, ducks, geese, cottontail rabbits, jackrabbits, fox squirrels

176

Nevada
Nevada Department of Fish and Game
Box 10678
Reno, Nevada 89510

> mule deer, elk, pronghorn antelope, bighorn sheep, cougar, ringneck pheasants, Hungarian partridges, chukar (G), sage grouse, blue grouse, Gambel's quail, California quail, mountain quail, cottontail rabbits, pigmy rabbits, jackrabbits, doves (G), ducks, geese

New Hampshire
New Hampshire Fish and Game Department
34 Bridge Street
Concord, New Hampshire 03301

> whitetail deer (G), black bear, wild boar, ringneck pheasants, ruffed grouse (G), woodcock, snipe, ducks, geese, gray squirrels, cottontail rabbits, snowshoe hares (G)

New Jersey
New Jersey Division of Fish, Game and Shellfisheries
State Labor Building
Box 1809
Trenton, New Jersey 08625

> whitetail deer, black bear, ringneck pheasants, bobwhite quail, ruffed grouse, woodcock, rails (G), ducks, geese, gray squirrels, cottontail rabbits

New Mexico
New Mexico Department of Game and Fish
State Capitol
Sante Fe, New Mexico 87501

> whitetail deer, mule deer (G), elk, pronghorn antelope, desert big-horn sheep, Barbary sheep, black bear, cougar, javelina, ringneck pheasants, blue grouse, prairie chickens, bobwhite quail (G), scaled quail (G), Gambel's quail (G), wild turkeys, doves (G), sandhill cranes, ducks, geese, tassel-eared squirrels, cottontail rabbits (G), jackrabbits (G)

New York
New York Department of Environmental Conservation
Division of Fish and Wildlife
Albany, New York 12201

> whitetail deer, black bear, ringneck pheasants, Hungarian partridges, bobwhite quail, ruffed grouse, wild turkeys, woodcock, rails, ducks,

geese, gray squirrels, cottontail rabbits, snowshoe hares

North Carolina
North Carolina Wildlife Resources Commission
P.O. Box 2919
Raleigh, North Carolina 27602
>whitetail deer, black bear, wild boar, bobwhite quail (G), ruffed grouse, wild turkeys, doves (G), rails, ducks (G), geese, gray squirrels, cottontail rabbits (G), marsh rabbits

North Dakota
North Dakota Game and Fish Department
2121 Lovett Avenue
Bismark, North Dakota 58501
>whitetail deer, mule deer, pronghorn antelope, ringneck pheasants, Hungarian partridges, ruffed grouse, sage grouse, sharptail grouse (G), wild turkeys, ducks (G), geese (G), gray and fox squirrels, cottontail rabbits (G), jackrabbits

Ohio
Division of Wildlife
Ohio Department of Natural Resources
1500 Dublin Road
Columbus, Ohio 43212
>whitetail deer, ringneck pheasants, Hungarian partridges, bobwhite quail, ruffed grouse (G), wild turkeys, woodcock, ducks, geese, gray and fox squirrels, cottontail rabbits

Oklahoma
Game Division
Oklahoma Department of Wildlife Conservation
1801 North Lincoln
Oklahoma City, Oklahoma 73105
>whitetail deer, ringneck pheasants, bobwhite quail (G), scaled quail, prairie chickens, wild turkeys, doves (G), ducks, geese, gray and fox squirrels, cottontail rabbits (G), jackrabbits

Oregon
Oregon Game Commission
P.O. Box 3503
Portland, Oregon 97208
>blacktail deer (G), mule deer, elk, pronghorn antelope, bighorn sheep, black bear (G), cougar, ringneck pheasants (G), Hungarian partridg-

es, chukar (G), bobwhite quail, California quail (G), mountain quail, blue grouse (G), ruffed grouse, sage grouse, wild turkeys, bandtail pigeons, doves (G), ducks (G), geese (G), cottontail rabbits, jackrabbits

Pennsylvania
Pennsylvania Game Commission
P.O. Box 1567
Harrisburg, Pennsylvania 17120

whitetail deer (G), black bear, ringneck pheasants, bobwhite quail, ruffed grouse, wild turkeys (G), woodcock, doves, ducks, geese, gray and fox squirrels, cottontail rabbits, snowshoe hares

Rhode Island
Rhode Island Department of Natural Resources
Veterans' Memorial Building
Providence, Rhode Island 02903

whitetail deer, ringneck pheasants, bobwhite quail, ruffed grouse, woodcock, doves, ducks(G), greese, gray squirrels, cottontail rabbits

South Carolina
South Carolina Wildlife Resources Department
Division of Game
1015 Main Street
Columbia, South Carolina 29202

whitetail deer (G), black bear, bobwhite quail (G), ruffed grouse, wild turkeys, doves (G), woodcock, rails, ducks, geese, gray and fox squirrels, cottontail rabbits (G)

South Dakota
South Dakota Department of Game, Fish and Parks
State Office Building
Pierre, South Dakota 57501

whitetail deer (G), mule deer, pronghorn antelope, mountain goats, ringneck pheasants (G), Hungarian partridges, bobwhite quail, sharptail grouse (G), prairie chickens, sage grouse, wild turkeys, sandhill cranes, ducks (G), geese (G), gray and fox squirrels, cottontail rabbits (G), jackrabbits

Tennessee
Tennessee Game and Fish Commission
P.O. Box 40747
Ellington Agricultural Center

Nashville, Tennessee
>whitetail deer, wild boar, bobwhite quail, ruffed grouse, wild turkeys, doves (G), ducks, geese, gray squirrels, cottontail rabbits, swamp rabbits

Texas

Texas Parks and Wildlife Commission
John J. Reagan Building
Austin, Texas 78701
>whitetail deer (G), mule deer, pronghorn antelope, elk, Aoudad sheep, javelina, black bear, exotic big game on private ranches, ringneck pheasants, prairie chickens, bobwhite quail (G), scaled quail (G), Gambel's quail, wild turkeys (G), doves (G), snipe, rails (G), ducks (G), geese (G), squirrels, cottontail rabbits (G), jackrabbits

Utah

Utah Division of Fish and Game
1596 W. N. Temple
Salt Lake City, Utah 84116
>mule deer (G), elk, moose, pronghorn antelope, desert bighorn sheep, buffalo, cougar, ringneck pheasants, Hungarian partridges, chukar (G), blue grouse, ruffed grouse, sage grouse, wild turkeys, doves, ducks, geese, squirrels, cottontail rabbits (G), jackrabbits

Vermont

Vermont Fish and Game Commission
Montpelier, Vermont 05602
>whitetail deer (G), black bear, ringneck pheasants, ruffed grouse (G), woodcock, ducks (G), geese, gray squirrels, cottontail rabbits, snowshoe hares (G)

Virginia

Virginia Commission of Game and Inland Fisheries
P.O. Box 11104
Richmond, Virginia 23230
>whitetail deer (G), black bear, Iranian pheasants, bobwhite quail (G), ruffed grouse, wild turkeys (G), doves, rails, ducks (G), geese, gray and fox squirrels, cottontail rabbits

Washington

Washington Department of Game
600 N. Capitol Way
Olympia, Washington 98501
>whitetail deer, mule deer, blacktail deer, elk, bighorn sheep, moun-

tain goats, black bear (G), cougar, ringneck pheasants, Hungarian partridges, chukar (G), ruffed grouse, blue grouse (G), spruce grouse, sage grouse, sharptail grouse, California quail, mountain quail, wild turkeys, bandtail pigeons (G), doves, ducks (G), geese, cottontail rabbits, jackrabbits, snowshoe hares (G)

West Virginia
West Virginia Department of Natural Resources
Division of Fish and Game
1800 Washington Street East
Charleston, West Virginia 25305
>whitetail deer (G), black bear, ringneck pheasants, ruffed grouse, bobwhite quail, wild turkeys (G), doves, ducks, geese, squirrels (G), cottontail rabbits (G)

Wisconsin
Division of Fish and Game
Wisconsin Department of Natural Resources
Box 450
Madison, Wisconsin 53701
>whitetail deer (G), black bear, ringneck pheasants, Hungarian partridges, ruffed grouse (G), woodcock, sharptail grouse, ducks, geese, gray and fox squirrels, cottontail rabbits, snowshoe hares

Wyoming
Wyoming Fish and Game Commission
P.O. Box 1589
Cheyenne, Wyoming 82001
>whitetail deer (G), mule deer (G), elk (G), moose, bighorn sheep, mountain goats, pronghorn antelope (G), black bear, grizzly bear, ringneck pheasants, Hungarian partridges (G), chukar (G), bobwhite quail, blue grouse, ruffed grouse, sharptail grouse, sage grouse (G), wild turkeys, ducks, geese, cottontail rabbits (G), jackrabbits, snowshoe hares

CANADA
Alberta
Fish and Game Division
Alberta Department of Lands and Forests
Natural Resources Building
Edmonton, Alberta
>whitetail deer, mule deer (G), elk, moose (G), mountain caribou, bighorn sheep, mountain goats, pronghorn antelope, black bear,

grizzly bear, cougar, ringneck pheasants (G), Hungarian partridges (G), sharptail grouse, ruffed grouse, spruce grouse, blue grouse, ptarmigan, ducks (G), geese, jackrabbits, snowshoe hares

British Columbia
Fish and Wildlife Branch
British Columbia Department of Recreation and Conservation
Parliament Buildings
Victoria, British Columbia
> whitetail deer, mule deer (G), blacktail deer (G), elk (G), moose (G), mountain caribou (G), bighorn sheep, Dall sheep, stone sheep (G), mountain goats (G), black bear (G), grizzly bear (G), cougar (G), wolves, wolverines, ringneck pheasants, Hungarian partridges, chukar, ruffed grouse, blue grouse (G), spruce grouse, ptarmigan, doves, bandtail pigeons (G), snipe, ducks (G), geese, snowshoe hares

Manitoba
Tourist Branch
Manitoba Department of Tourism, Recreation and Cultural Affairs
408 Norquay Building
Winnipeg, Manitoba
> whitetail deer (G), moose (G), woodland caribou (G), elk, black bear (G), Hungarian partridges, ruffed grouse (G), spruce grouse, sharptail grouse (G), ptarmigan, snipe, ducks (G), geese (G), jackrabbits, snowshoe hares

New Brunswick
New Brunswick Travel Bureau
P.O. Box 1030
Fredericton, New Brunswick
> whitetail deer (G), moose, black bear (G), ruffed grouse (G), spruce grouse, woodcock (G), ducks, geese, snowshoe hares (G)

Newfoundland and Labrador
Newfoundland Tourist Development Office
Confederation Building
St. John's, Newfoundland
> moose (G), woodland caribou (G), black bear, ruffed grouse, ptarmigan (G), snipe (G), ducks (G), geese, snowshoe hares (G)

Northwest Territories
Travel Arctic
Yellowknife, Northwest Territories
> moose (G), barren ground caribou (G), Dall sheep (G), mountain goats, buffalo (G), black bear (G), grizzly bear (G), polar bear (G), wolves, ruffed grouse (G), blue grouse, spruce grouse, sharptail grouse ptarmigan, snipe, ducks (G), geese, snowshoe hares (G), Arctic hares

Nova Scotia
Division of Wildlife Conservation
Nova Scotia Department of Lands and Forests
Kentville, Nova Scotia
> whitetail deer (G), moose, black bear, ringneck pheasants, Hungarian partridges, ruffed grouse (G), woodcock, ducks (G), geese, snowshoe hares

Ontario
Public Relations Branch
Ontario Ministry of Industry and Tourism
900 Bay Street
Toronto, Ontario
> whitetail deer, moose (G), black bear (G), ringneck pheasants, Hungarian partridges, bobwhite quail, ruffed grouse (G), spruce grouse, sharptail grouse, ptarmigan, woodcock (G), ducks (G), geese (G), gray squirrels, cottontail rabbits, snowshoe hares (G), European hares

Prince Edward Island
Wildlife Division
P.E.I. Department of Tourist Development
Charlottetown, Prince Edward Island
> Hungarian partridges, ruffed grouse (G), woodcock, snipe (G), ducks (G), geese, snowshoe hares

Quebec
Tourist Branch
Quebec Department of Tourism, Fish and Game
930 St. Foy Street
Quebec City, Quebec
> whitetail deer, moose (G), caribou (G), black bear (G), ruffed grouse (G), spruce grouse, ptarmigan, woodcock (G), snipe (G), ducks (G), geese (G), cottontail rabbits, snowshoe hares (G)

183

Saskatchewan
Tourist Branch
Saskatchewan Department of Industry and Commerce
S.P.C. Building
Regina, Saskatchewan
>whitetail deer (G), mule deer, moose (G), woodland caribou, black bear (G), ringneck pheasants, Hungarian partridges (G), ruffed grouse (G), spruce grouse, snipe, ducks (G), geese (G), jackrabbits, snowshoe hares (G)

Yukon
Director
Yukon Game Department
Box 2703
Whitehorse, Yukon
>moose (G), caribou (G), Dall sheep (G), stone sheep, mountain goats, black bear (G), grizzly bear (G), ruffed grouse (G), blue grouse, spruce grouse, sharptail grouse, ptarmigan, ducks (G), geese, snowshoe hares (G)

MEXICO
Director General de Fauna Silvestre
S.A.G.
Aquiles Serdan No. 28 — 70 Piso
Mexico 3, D.F., Mexico
>whitetail deer (G), mule deer (G), Brocket deer, desert bighorn sheep, javelina (G), white-lipped peccary (G), black bear, bobwhite quail (G), scaled quail (G), Mearn's quail (G), Gambel's quail (G), tinamou, chachalca, curassow, crested guan, wild turkeys (G), doves (G), pigeons (G), ducks (G), geese (G), squirrels, cottontail rabbits (G), jackrabbits

APPENDIX

Conservation, Wildlife, and Firearms Organizations

1. National Wildlife Federation, 1412 — 16th Street N.W., Washington, D.C. 20036 (conservation and sportsmen's organization)

2. Canadian Nature Federation, 46 Elgin Street, Ottawa, Ontario K1P 5K6 (conservation organization)

3. Canadian Wildlife Federation, 1419 Carling Avenue, Ottawa, Ontario K1Z 7L7

4. National Audubon Society, 950 — 3rd Avenue, New York, New York 10022 (conservation organization)

5. The Sierra Club, 1050 Mills Tower, San Francisco, California 94104 (conservation organization)

6. The Wilderness Society, 729 — 15th Street N.W., Washington, D.C. 20005 (conservation organization)

7. National Rifle Association of America, 1600 Rhode Island Avenue N.W., Washington, D.C. 20036 (sportsmen's organization)

8. The Isaak Walton League, 1800 North Kent Street, Arlington, Virginia 22209 (conservation and sportsmen's organization)

9. Ducks Unlimited, P.O. Box 66300, Chicago, Illinois 60666 (conservation and wildlife management organization)

10. Boone and Crockett Club, Carnegie Museum, 4400 Forbes Avenue, Pittsburgh, Pennsylvania 15213 (conservation and sportsmen's organization — major interests in big game management and in keeping trophy records of North American big game)

ACKNOWLEDGEMENTS

My thanks to the Ontario Ministry of Natural Resources for diagram on page 59 and to the Canadian Industries Limited for the diagrams on pages 12, 13, 21, 22, 23.

Many thanks to Mrs. Mafalda Hart and Mrs. B. O'Krafka for their work in typing the manuscript.

And most of all, thanks to my wife, Alyson, who put up with me while I wrote this book, and worked as hard as I did.

PHOTO CREDITS

I thank the following agencies and individuals for allowing me to reproduce the photographs in this book:
Nebraska Game and Parks Commission, photos, 1, 5, 6; Ontario Ministry of Industry and Tourism, photos 3, 15, 19, 23; Ontario Ministry of Natural Resources, photos 9, 11; Georgia Fish and Game Commission, photos 7, 8; U.S. Bureau of Sport Fisheries and Wildlife, photos 10, 12; Information Canada Phototheque, photos 16, 18, 21, 25; Wyoming Game and Fish Department, photo 17; Peter Tasker, photo 20; New Mexico Department of Game and Fish, photo 26; Texas Park and Wildlife Department, photo 22; Jerome J. Knap, photos 2, 4, 13, 14, 27.